2

GOVERNMENTAL METHODS OF ADJUSTING LABOR DISPUTES

In North America and Australasia

STUDIES IN HISTORY, ECONOMICS AND PUBLIC LAW

EDITED BY THE FACULTY OF POLITICAL SCIENCE
OF COLUMBIA UNIVERSITY

Volume CXXIII] [Number 2

Whole Number 271

GOVERNMENTAL METHODS OF ADJUSTING LABOR DISPUTES

IN NORTH AMERICA AND AUSTRALASIA

BY

TING TSZ KO

AMS PRESS
NEW YORK

COLUMBIA UNIVERSITY
STUDIES IN THE
SOCIAL SCIENCES

271

The Series was formerly known as
Studies in History, Economics and Public Law

Reprinted with the permission of Columbia University Press
From the edition of 1926, New York
First AMS EDITION published 1968
Manufactured in the United States of America

Library of Congress Catalogue Card Number: 68-57570

AMS PRESS, INC.
NEW YORK, N.Y. 10003

Dedicated

TO MY INSPIRING PROFESSORS AND ESTEEMED FRIENDS OF THREE NOBLE INSTITUTIONS OF LEARNING—THE NATIONAL UNIVERSITY OF PEKING, THE LINGNAN UNIVERSITY AT CANTON, AND COLUMBIA UNIVERSITY IN THE CITY OF NEW YORK

CONTENTS

PAGE

CHAPTER I

INTRODUCTION 9

CHAPTER II

METHODS OF ADJUSTING LABOR DISPUTES IN THE DIFFERENT STATES OF THE UNITED STATES

I. Tentative Mediation 14
II. Positive Mediation 17
III. Voluntary Arbitration 23
IV. Compulsory Investigation 26
V. Obligatory Arbitration 28
VI. Quasi-Judicial Adjudication 30

CHAPTER III

METHODS OF ADJUSTING RAILROAD LABOR DISPUTES IN THE UNITED STATES

I. Positive Mediation and Voluntary Arbitration—Policy before 1914 54
II. Legislative Settlement and Wage Board Adjustment—Policy during the World War 73
III. Advisory Determination—Policy since 1920 82

CHAPTER IV

COMPULSORY INVESTIGATION IN CANADA

I. Antecedents of the Industrial Disputes Investigation Act . . 103
II. Machinery of the Act 105
III. Interpretation of the Act 108
IV. General Results and Estimates of the System 114
V. The Act Declared Unconstitutional 119

PAGE

CHAPTER V

Compulsory Arbitration in New Zealand

I. The Machinery of Compulsory Arbitration in New Zealand . . 129
II. General Results of the Experiment 135
III. Merits and Demerits of the System 143

CHAPTER VI

Compulsory Arbitration in Australia

I. Compulsory Arbitration in South Australia and Other States. 147
II. Wage Board Adjustment in Victoria 152
III. Compulsory Arbitration in New South Wales 159
IV. Wage Board Adjustment and Compulsory Arbitration in Queensland 181
V. Compulsory Arbitration in the Australian Commonwealth. . 189

CHAPTER VII

Conclusion

I. Recapitulation 200
II. The Principles and Problems of Voluntary Arbitration . . . 202
III. The Principles and Problems of Compulsory Investigation. . 206
IV. The Principles and Problems of Compulsory Arbitration . . 209

Index 221

CHAPTER I

Introduction

Human relations correspond in complexity to the many forms of human activities. Human society has long been one of interdependence. Especially in the present industrial world, where networks of railroads facilitate the rapid flow of transportation, where fleets of vessels carry on world-wide commerce and where millions of factories shelter countless machines and hosts of men and women toiling at their assigned tasks, interdependence has become one of the chief characteristics of human relations. The introduction of machinery necessitates a minute subdivision of labor which in turn increases the degree of interdependence between men and men as well as between one factory and other factories, between one manufacturing unit and the rest of the business units.

In this industrial society where the interests of its constituents are so intimately interwoven, the importance of labor can scarcely be exaggerated. Especially in the key industries, continuous operation of which is an absolute necessity, the human factor is undoubtedly of primary importance.

The many volumes of literature on industrial relations all recognize the simple fact that any conflict between employers and employees involves social loss. Any remedy which lessens the possibility of industrial warfare, must be, therefore, a contribution towards the promotion of public welfare. Economists and sociologists are still engaged in the search for some solution of the Labor Problem, but just as in medical science no panacea has yet been discovered for human illness, in like manner, no panacea is yet of any avail for industrial illness.

In the following monograph, I propose no panacea. My task is to describe the different governmental systems for adjusting industrial controversies between employers and employees in North America and Australasia. I shall endeavor to point out their significance and their relations, their fundamental principles and their specific problems.

The divergent economic conditions and different theories of government prevailing in different countries or in different sections of the same country, naturally lead to the formulation of dissimilar policies. The governmental methods for the adjustment of labor disputes naturally take different shapes inasmuch as they are subject to the influences of dissimilar material circumstances and of diverse political theories of government.

The policies for labor adjustment, within the scope of this essay, group themselves into no less than eleven distinct types, when classified from the standpoint of the degree of power exercised by the government. The eleven types of polices are, namely: (1) *conciliation*, (2) *tentative mediation*, (3) *positive mediation*, (4) *voluntary arbitration*, (5) *advisory determination*, (6) *wage board adjustment*, (7) *compulsory investigation*, (8) *obligatory arbitration*, (9) *compulsory arbitration*, (10) *quasi-judicial adjudication*, (11) *legislative settlement*.

Conciliation, strictly speaking, means the adjustment of differences between two disputants without outside assistance. In this method the government plays no part. The terms conciliation and mediation, however, are often used interchangeably. But it is better to make the distinction and adhere to its strict usage.

Tentative mediation exists when a government begins to take steps toward intervening in labor disputes, by inquiring into their causes and bringing the warring parties to a settlement, but exercises no active interference, nor sets up any special agency for the purpose. *Positive mediation* also means the bringing of the disputant parties together for the peaceful settlement of a controversy. The government in this case sets up a special tribunal for the purpose and the officials of the tribunal are entrusted with special duties to mediate in labor disputes.

Broadly speaking, positive mediation includes arbitration. On the other hand, arbitration differs from mediation in that the former calls for an authoritative settlement of disputes while the latter limits itself to informal intervention by bringing the disputant parties to an agreement. Arbitration, however, consists of two forms, *voluntary* and *compulsory*. When arbitration results from the willingness and free choice of both disputant parties to submit their differences to a third party for settlement, it is termed voluntary arbitration. Whether or not the acceptance of the award is obligatory, arbitration is voluntary when agreement to enter into arbitration depends entirely upon the choice of both disputants to take the course. Arbitration becomes compulsory, when the law compels the disputants to submit their controversies to the judgment of a government tribunal whose decision is binding and enforceable.

Advisory determination, while it requires the disputants to submit their controversies to a board for adjustment, gives the parties the right to accept or reject the decision of the board. The award of the board may be final but disobedience or violation of the award is not criminal.

Wage board adjustment, as it was originally designed, was a form of round-table discussion. But gradually it has taken shape as a form of compulsory arbitration. Under this system, the government can order any industry or trade to form a wage board and make adjustment as directed by the government. Usually employers and employees are equally represented on the board, and in case of deadlock in regard to the selection of the chairman, the government appoints the chairman for the board.

Compulsory investigation requires the parties to a dispute to produce books and documents, to testify under oath, and to discharge other obligations necessary for thorough-going investigation. The most significant feature of compulsory investigation is that which prohibits strikes and lockouts before or during the proceedings of the investigating board. Neither the right of the employees to strike, nor the right of the employers to discharge is forfeited by law, but the exercise of these rights is suspended for a certain time. Unlike compulsory arbitration, in which the procedure undertakes to compel a settlement of the dispute by forcing the parties to abide by the decision of a board or court, compulsory investigation aims to publish the facts concerning a dispute and by means of these facts to guide public opinion to bring pressure to bear on the uncompromising party, and thus facilitate agreement.

Obligatory arbitration and *quasi-judicial adjudication*, however, closely resemble compulsory arbitration. The difference between obligatory and compulsory arbitration is that the former provides that in the course of a dispute, when one of the disputants proposes arbitration, the other disputant party should accept the proposal, while the latter demands the submission of a case to the authoritative settlement by a court even when both disputants are reluctant to surrender their rights. In the larger sense of the term, quasi-judicial adjudication is identical with compulsory arbitration, for, in theory, both systems compel the warring parties to submit their grievances to a government tribunal for adjudication. But, technically, there is one minor difference which sets a line of demarcation between these two methods. A compulsory arbitration court is usually composed of representatives of the three parties interested — employers, employees and the public. Quasi-judicial adjudication denies partisan representation. All the members of a quasi-judicial court are representatives of the government. The degree of power exercised by the government in the case of quasi-judicial determination, in theory, is, therefore, somewhat greater than that in compulsory arbitration. In practice, however, compulsory arbitration has so widened its scope of action that it has come to mean compulsory labor legislation.

Legislative settlement means the passage of a law in order to compel settlement of a dispute. When a dispute has reached an acute stage, the government under the pressure of circumstances may prevent a final deadlock by passing a law to impose terms upon the warring parties.

Boiled down to a few general terms, this treatise deals chiefly with four principal types of governmental methods of adjusting labor disputes, namely, positive mediation, voluntary arbitration, compulsory investigation and compulsory arbitration.

CHAPTER II

Methods of Adjusting Labor Disputes in the Different States of the United States

Among the forty-eight states of the Union, thirty-two have enacted mediation, investigation and arbitration laws of one kind or another. The thirty-two states are, namely, Alabama, California, Colorado, Connecticut, Georgia, Idaho, Illinois, Indiana, Iowa, Kansas, Louisiana, Maine, Maryland, Massachusetts, Minnesota, Montana, Nebraska, Nevada, New Hampshire, New Jersey, New York, Ohio, Oregon, Oklahoma, Pennsylvania, South Carolina, South Dakota, Texas, Utah, Vermont, Washington and Wisconsin.

Many of these states, however, create no state agencies, and only a few of the existing state agencies are in active service. In Texas, Nebraska and Maryland, for example, boards of mediation and arbitration are created only when industrial disputes arise, and the boards cease to exist when adjustments are made. In some states the law provides that a permanent board should be created, yet this section of the law has not always been carried out, even though the law has been in existence for many years. Minnesota is a case in point. Minnesota passed its arbitration law in 1895 but it was not until 1917 that the law was in actual operation. Since 1920, it has fallen back into its previous inactivity. In some states the arbitration laws have been so obsolete that state officials, who are responsible for the administration of the laws, are ignorant even of the existence of the laws. An Indiana chairman of the industrial board said that the arbitration law in his state was so obsolete that he was unable to tell whether there was such a law. " . . . If there is an arbitration law in this state, it has been unused for a number of years and there is a possibility that none exists . . ." As a matter of fact, Indiana has had an arbitration law since 1897.

Some states have either found their arbitration board of little use and have abolished the agency or repealed the law entirely. Illinois, which placed its arbitration law on its statute book as early as in 1895, found its state board of arbitration unnecessary, and abolished the board in 1917. The duties of the board were then transferred to the industrial commission. Since the reorganization, any accounts of the mediation work of the commission can hardly be found. The commission gives the explanation that it has been its theory that the less publicity given to a controversy, as far as mediation is concerned, the better is the chance of successful adjustment. "Many controversies have been settled, of which the public knows nothing, and in many cases the parties to the controversy and other parties who have assisted in bringing about a settlement, do not desire publicity."[1]

The experiment of arbitration in California supplies the best example of inactiveness. California first enacted its arbitration law in 1891 and three months after the enactment, a board was appointed. But the board remained so entirely inactive that the Tenth Biennial Report of the California Bureau of Labor Statistics was obliged to state (page 134): "there is no record of any work ever having been done by the Board, or any report having been published by it as to its work." Dr.

[1] Illinois Department of Labor, *Third Annual Report*, 1919–1920, p. 70.

Leonard W. Hatch, Statistician of New York, in his book *Government Industrial Arbitration*, U. S. Bureau of Labor Statistics, Bulletin No. 60, p. 613, accepted the statement of the Bureau and also quoted a statement from the California Commissioner of Labor in 1905 that the Board had continued in existence for only a year and never had a successor. But as a matter of fact, on October 13, 1892, the Board submitted a short report to Governor H. Markham, showing that it had acted upon two cases in 1891, and recommending an amendment to the law for the establishment of a permanent board. Another short report of the Board, dated September 3, 1894, said: "The undersigned commissioners of the State Board of Arbitration, in submitting this, their second report, desire to say that the Commission was not called upon, since date of this last report, to settle any differences arising between employers and their employees, although there have been occasions in which their mediation might have been beneficial."[1] All these errors show that the laws were in these instances of no practical importance. Furthermore, in 1921, the Californian Legislature found the law of so small significance that the law was repealed.

Under these circumstances, the following survey attempts to cover only the nature and results of the state laws arbitrarily yet logically chosen as representative types to illustrate the different methods of adjusting labor disputes in the different states of the United States. On the basis of the degree of power exercised by the government, a classification of the state laws in this field divides them into six general groups.

[1] California State Office: *Report of the Commissioners of the State Board of Arbitration, Sacramento, 1892–1894.*

I. TENTATIVE MEDIATION

In the loosest form of governmental intervention in labor disputes, that is, tentative mediation, the government exerts no more power than is necessary to facilitate their adjustment through the offer of its services to the disputants. In Georgia, which is the only state in this class, the commissioner of labor possesses merely the power to inquire into the causes of strikes and lock-outs, in an effort to bring about an amicable settlement. He is not authorized to arbitrate, nor is he empowered to investigate.

The ineffectiveness of this type of mediation can easily be seen, and for this reason, the Commissioner of Commerce and Labor recommended that the law should be changed. In 1912, the year following, the creation of the commission of commerce and labor, the commissioner made a recommendation to the effect that an arbitration law similar to the Erdman Act[1] was greatly needed. In 1913, as well as in the three or four following years, the same recommendation appeared in the annual reports of the commission to the governor of that state. In 1918, a measure providing for arbitration was approved in the senate but was lost in the house. Although the recommendation for an arbitration law shows a tendency toward a more active participation in industrial disputes, accounts of the mediation work of the commission are not available.

II. POSITIVE MEDIATION

The next group is that of positive mediation in which a state agency is empowered to mediate and when mediation fails, the mediators may offer arbitration to the contending parties for adjustment. But if either one of

[1] *Cf. infra*, pp. 57-58.

the parties refuses mediation or arbitration, the government has to let the dispute take its own course. This type of mediation finds its best examples in three states, namely, Pennsylvania, New York and Ohio.

Pennsylvania first inaugurated its system of mediation in 1883, and the mediation work was carried on by the board of mediation and arbitration. But the present Bureau of Mediation was organized only in June, 1913. In its report for 1914, the Bureau stated that it had been confined in its efforts to conciliation and mediation rather than to arbitration. The reports of the Pennsylvania Department of Labor and Industries attempt to give brief accounts of some of the disputes, the dates and places of their occurrence, their magnitude and their duration. But there are no statistics published showing the number of cases settled by conciliation, by mediation or by arbitration. The figures available for an examination of the Bureau's work cover the period from 1916 to 1919. During this four-year period, there were 1615 strikes reported to the Bureau, the Bureau intervened in 754 cases and of these 736 cases were settled. This by no means implies, however, that the successful settlements were attributable entirely to the efforts of the Bureau. It indicates that in the disputes, in connection with which the Bureau offered its services, through its efforts in conjunction with the cooperation of other agencies mutual agreements were arrived at by the disputants.

During 1921, there were 1174 strikes reported in Pennsylvania. In addition thirty-six were carried over from the previous year, making a total of 1210 cases. In these strikes, the Bureau was active in 571 cases, but no record was kept of the strikes actually settled through the efforts of its mediators. It would be unfair to hold the two or three men in the Bureau responsible for the failure to adjust such a large proportion of the disputes. It is a physical impossibility for so few men to mediate in every dispute, for while they are busily engaged in negotiations for the settlement of disputes in one part of the state, disputes often occur at the same time in another part. The number of mediators is not sufficient to cope with such a situation as not infrequently arises.

The New York mediation and arbitration law first came into operation in 1886, and the New York Board of Mediation and Arbitration has been considered as one of the most active boards. The operation of the system, however, made a poor beginning. During the first year (seven months) of the board's existence, there were 350 strikes and lockouts (whole year), but the board intervened in only 7 cases, among which 6 cases were acted upon after the strikes and lockouts had occurred and in only one case was there a peaceful settlement. This inaction was due to the rigid provision of the law that the board was not empowered to conduct mediation or arbitration upon its own initiative. The parties to the controversy, if willing to submit their differences to the board, were required to send a written application to the board before it could render its services.

After an experiment of seven months, the law of May 18, 1886, was amended by the act of March 10, 1887. This amending act vested the board with power to mediate in cases where disputes between employers and employees threatened a strike or lockout. The board was further empowered to conduct investigations into the causes of any labor controversies. These changes brought the board into active service. From 1887 to 1900, the board acted upon 402 cases of which 345 cases were investigated upon its own initiative. Of the 402 cases, 135 cases were acted upon as a result of preliminary investigation, and 267 were acted upon through positive intervention. Moreover, of the 267 cases, there were 112 which resulted in a settlement and only the remaining 155 cases were failures. However, from the date of the enactment of the law (1886) to the time of the reorganization of the board (1900) there were only 19 cases which were adjusted successfully without a strike or lockout taking place.

The New York experiment may be reviewed from another angle—the method of adjustment. From 1901 to 1925, there were 4382 disputes reported to the Board of Mediation and Arbitration.[1] Of these disputes, 1826 cases were adjusted by direct negotiations, that is by conciliation, 645 cases by mediation and only 77 cases by arbitration. The remaining 1834 were either deadlocked or adjusted by other means. All these figures tend to show that mediation as a method for adjusting industrial controversies is far more frequently used than arbitration, so far as the New York experiment goes, and conciliation is a still more adequate measure than mediation.

Ohio first enacted its arbitration law in 1893, but it has given up arbitration and instead it has adopted the policy of mediation. During the first seven years of its arbitration experiment, the board intervened in 160 cases, 21 of which were mediated before strikes and lockouts occurred, and 139 after strikes and lockouts had taken place. During the same period, in only 6 cases was peaceful settlement effected without strikes and lockouts, and only 53 strikes and lockouts were settled.

[1] *New York Department of Labor*, *Annual Reports*, 1901–1925.

From 1893 to 1900, there were 678 strikes and lockouts reported in Ohio, and the board took action in 103 cases and settled 35, that is, 33.9 per cent.

The board encountered three obstacles which hampered its success: the difficulty of forming a local board of arbitration, the failure of the local board to cooperate with the state board, and the frequent refusal of the employers and employees to submit their cases for arbitration. In almost all of its reports, the Ohio board complained that while every year it exerted itself to bring about settlements in times of strike, in some instances the employers refused to submit their differences to arbitration and in other instances the employees declined the services of the board and refused to discuss grievances.

The difficulty in forming the local board centered on the question of compensation for the arbitrators. In its annual report of 1904 (page 10), the board said: "While the law provides for such local arbitrators, there is no definite provision for their compensation unless such payment is approved by the city or county authorities. . . ." The board went on to show that in two instances where local boards of arbitration were selected on their advice, and where valuable service was performed, "the city council and county commissioners refused to pay for such service." This, in the opinion of the board, was a bad policy, but what was still worse was that in some cases where the employers and employees had agreed to submit their grievances to a local board of arbitration, the State board was "unable to secure the service of local arbitrators, owing to the fact that their pay was not assured."

The report of the board in 1905, as well as previous reports, indicated that the failure of the mayor or local authorities to give official notice of the controversies to the board was one of the great obstacles to its successful administration Records for the period between 1895 and 1903 indicate that only twenty-nine cases had been reported by the local authorities. Consequently, the work of the board at this early period was greatly limited and its failure was justifiable.

The work of the board in recent years has been negligible. The last statistical account of the board's work was that of 1914–1916, a period of two and a half years. During this period, the board acted on twenty-six disputes, and of these twenty-six cases, eleven were settled, as a result of the board's mediation, including one case which resulted in arbitration.

In spite of the inactivity of the board from the viewpoint of practical result, the board has described a procedure of mediation which deserves attention. It says that the procedure of mediation pursued in Ohio has been one of indirect negotiation. Representatives of parties to a dispute have seldom been brought together in conference for direct negotiations, but instead, confidential conferences are usually held with one party, then with the other party. Through these confidential conferences, the mediators learn the position of both sides and secure a basis for adjustment. The terms proposed to either party come not from the parties in dispute, but from the mediators in whose opinion the settlement should be satisfactory to both sides. The proposals are made not as terms imposed upon the parties, but with the understanding that unless the parties accept the proposals the terms are to be withdrawn and each side will be in exactly the same position as previous to the mediation.

The merit of this scheme lies in the fact that indirect negotiations are less likely to kindle the anger of the party approached by unpleasant arguments or by arousing hostile feelings towards its opponent. When both parties maintain a calm attitude, agreement is easier to be reached than otherwise. The great defect of the plan, however, is obvious. Very few men can command the confidence of two warring parties, and those who possess such great ability and prestige may not be willing to accept positions as mediators. But whenever mediators can gain the confidence of both sides, the plan is undoubtedly valuable.

III. VOLUNTARY ARBITRATION

Voluntary arbitration is best exemplified in Massachusetts. The Massachusetts law, however, provides not voluntary arbitration alone, but government investigation as well. In this form of government intervention, the State recognizes the right of the individual to accept or reject the method of arbitration, but it imposes upon the party which refuses to arbitrate the responsibility of justifying itself in the eyes of the public. By means of the publication of the findings by the arbitration board, the government tries to bring public opinion to bear upon the uncompromising party.

There are other features of the law which mark it as a distinct type by itself. The Massachusetts law goes a step further than mere voluntary arbitration. It requires "a promise to continue in business or at work without any lockout or strike until the decision of the board, if made within three weeks after the date of filing the application."[1] The law does not prohibit the right of the employees to strike, nor the right of the employers to lockout. It provides, however, that when application has been made, the parties involved should defer the use of these rights for a certain period of time.

[1] *General Law of Massachusetts, 1921*, chapter 150, sec. 6.

Another distinctive feature of the law is an amendment added in 1910 which provides that an employer, who, during the continuance of a strike or other labor trouble, publicly advertises for employees to fill the places of the strikers, must explicitly mention in the advertisement that a strike has been in existence. Any violation of this provision is punishable by a fine of not exceeding one hundred dollars for each offence. In 1916 (chapter 89) this section of the law was amended so as to read as follows: "Any person, firm, association or corporation violating any provision of this act shall upon complaint of and after investigation by the state board of labor and industries, be punished by a fine not exceeding one hundred dollars for each offense."

The section providing for advertisement for employees during the existence of a strike had already been greatly modified by an amendment in 1912 which provided that the requirement of the section would cease to be operative when the State board of "conciliation and arbitration" had determined that the business of the employer in respect to which the strike had occurred, was being carried on in the normal manner to the usual extent, and that the board was to determine this state of affairs upon the application of the employer. In 1916, this section was further amended so that the determination of this state of affairs as to the normal manner shall be decided by the board, "but only after a full hearing at which all persons involved shall be entitled to be heard and represented by counsel."

The Massachusetts experiment shows that voluntary arbitration, combined with compulsory investigation, is fairly effective. The result of mediation and arbitration during the first four months of its existence in 1886 duplicated the experience of New York, since the board remained for all practical purposes idle. Only four cases were acted upon, and intervention in two of these cases failed. The very same provision, which limited the jurisdiction of the New York Board and caused its inaction, was responsible for the initial failure of the Massachusetts Board. In a similar fashion, however, the Massachusetts law was amended in 1887, cancelling the original section which required an application from one or both parties to the controversy before the board could take action. Under the amended law, the board was given the power to intervene upon its own motion for the purpose of settling differences by mediation, arbitration and investigation. This change, of course, increased the activity of the board. In 1887, twenty-one cases were acted upon, ten of which were taken up upon the initiative of the board. Again, in 1888, intervention was made in forty-one cases of which sixteen were taken up upon the initiative of the board.

The period from 1887 to 1900 is most adequate for a comparison of the work of the Massachusetts and the New York boards. During these thirteen years, the Massachusetts board acted upon 450 cases, of which 373 cases became the subjects of positive mediation. Of the 373 cases, 213 resulted in a settlement and only 160 were failures. The comparative success of the board can be demonstrated more clearly by the number of disputes settled peacefully without strikes and lockouts and the number of strikes and lockouts settled after they had occurred. During the same period (1887–1900), the board settled successfully 104 cases without strikes and lockouts, and 109 actual strikes and lockouts were settled through the services of the board.

The Massachusetts board is perhaps the most successful of its kind in the United States. However, the percentage of strikes and lockouts settled, compared with the total number of strikes and lockouts from 1887 to 1900, is not entirely satisfactory. During this period of thirteen years, 1458 strikes and lockouts occurred and the board settled only 109, that is 7.4 per cent.

A great change in the administration of the law occurred in 1919 in the transfer of the functions of the Board of Conciliation and Arbitration to the Department of Labor and Industries. From this time on, the functions of the board have been vested in three associate commissioners of the Department of Labor and Industries. The work of the board after its reorganization is still encouraging. From 1920 to 1924 inclusive, there were 2432 cases submitted to the board and the board had rendered 1700 arbitration decisions.[1] The remaining cases were adjusted either by recommendations, accepted in lieu of decisions, or by conciliation. Some of the cases were either abandoned or withdrawn.

IV. COMPULSORY INVESTIGATION

Compulsory investigation, while resting on the support of public opinion for the final enforcement of awards, compels contending parties to submit their differences to an official investigation before strikes or lockouts may occur. The Colorado Industrial Relation Act of 1915 patterned after the Canadian Industrial Investigation Act, pursues this policy of prohibiting strikes before or during investigation. The State Industrial Commission possesses power to make investigation with respect to any matter of employment and has jurisdiction over all labor disputes in the State. The commission may at any reasonable time enter any building,

[1] *Massachusetts Department of Labor and Industries, Annual Reports*, 1920-1924.

mine or workshop and inspect material and appliances therein. Employers and employees are required to give to the commission "at least thirty days' prior written notice of an intended change affecting conditions of employment or with respect to wages or hours."[1] For the purpose of determining differences, it has power to force the attendance of witnesses, to administer oaths and require the production of books, papers and documents. Violation of the act subjects the offending party to a fine or imprisonment or both.

Since the enactment of the law in August, 1915, up to December, 1922, there were 1011 cases filed with the commission for intervention. Most of these cases were concerned with controversies over wages. But only a small proportion of these cases was settled by the awards of the commission. There have been numerous refusals to give thirty days' notice to the commission before the employers altered the wage scales. Three great strikes of outstanding importance occurred in Colorado in 1919. These were the coal strike, the steel strike and the tramway strike. But no notice was given to the commission before the strikes began, although two of these strikes were of national character rather than local disputes.

The most significant case, from the standpoint of the operation of the Industrial Relation Act, was the investigation by the commission of the Denver Tramway case, 1920. This case demonstrates the ineffectiveness of the commission's award. The War Labor Board had granted a wage scale of forty-eight cents per hour to the tramway workers. A contract based upon this scale was then entered into between the Denver Tramway Company and its employees. The contract, besides the wage and

[1] *Colorado Compiled Laws*, 1921, chap. LXXIX, sec. 4353.

other provisions, specified that in case dispute should arise concerning the terms of the contract, the matter should be submitted to arbitration. This anticipated disagreement did occur, and consequently, an arbitration was held. The result of the arbitration was in favor of a ten-cent per hour increase in wages. The company then proceeded to cancel the contract entirely.

The matter was brought to the attention of the commission. The commission after an investigation decided in favor of the company's contention that it could not increase wages above the old rate of forty-eight cents per hour. At the same time, the commission recommended to the city authorities an increase of street car fares in case the higher wage scale were to be adopted. The city administration ignored the recommendation and brought suit in the District Court of Denver compelling the company to continue operation of the street car service and also restraining the employees from striking. The employees, however, ordered a strike and a complete cessation in the operation of the street cars occurred. But the strike was lost after the intervention of Federal troops which safeguarded the importation of strike breakers.

The commission is only an administrative body. The enforcement of the law ultimately depends upon the district or state courts. The commission, however, would fulfill an important duty if it would strive to enlighten public opinion.

V. OBLIGATORY ARBITRATION

Obligatory arbitration exists in the United States only in South Carolina, and is applicable only to street railways. The South Carolina statute[1] provides that when

[1] *South Carolina Statutes*, Act No. 589, 1922.

differences between employer and employees arise, the parties shall submit their controversy to arbitration upon the invitation of either party to the controversy. "The employer and employees shall submit such matters of difference to a board of arbitration, if either party, that is, the employer or employees, make request therefor."[1]

This provision naturally leads to a supplementary provision as to the selection of arbitrators, for the party which refuses to submit its case to arbitration may get around the law by a wilful disagreement with the opposing party in regard to the selection of the arbitrators. For the purpose of making the obligatory clause practicable, the law contains a further provision that within five days the two arbitrators chosen by the respective parties should choose the third and that in the event of deadlock, the mayor of the city in which the street railway is located shall act as the third arbitrator.

Nevertheless, the law would be still incomplete without a further provision requiring the parties to select their respective arbitrators. To this end, the law provides that if within five days a party fails to name its arbitrator, then the judge of the Circuit Court shall name the arbitrator for the party.[2]

The significance of these provisions is that they make the law practically a type of compulsory arbitration. The act clearly manifests its compulsory character at two points: the selection of the mayor to be the third arbitrator in the event of a deadlock, and the empowering of the judge of the Circuit Court to choose an arbitrator for a party in case of refusal to arbitrate. This method exposes the system to the immense influence of politics. Realizing this danger to the successful operation of the

[1] *South Carolina Statutes:* Act No. 589, 1922, sec. 1.

[2] *Ibid.*, sec. 2.

law, the framers of the statute limit the jurisdiction of the law to counties in which there are incorporated cities the population of which according to the last census is not less than thirty thousand and not more than fifty thousand.

The act has never once been invoked since its enactment. The result would have been more important and interesting had the act been in active operation.

VI. QUASI-JUDICIAL ADJUDICATION—THE KANSAS PLAN

The Kansas Industrial Relations Act of 1920 has seven distinguishing features:

First, it declares that essential industries such as those concerned with food, clothing, fuel and transportation, are from their nature vested with a public interest, and therefore, are made subject to the supervision of the state.

Second, it creates an industrial court, which is vested with power and jurisdiction to hear and make decision on all controversies which may arise and hinder the continuous operation of such industries.

Third, it declares it unlawful for any person, firm or corporation to discharge any employee because of the fact that such employee may have signed a complaint to the tribunal; and also makes it unlawful for any two or more persons, confederating together, to injure any person, firm or corporation by boycott, picketing or other means on account of the fact that such person, firm, or corporation has invoked the jurisdiction of the Industrial Court.

Fourth, it declares it unlawful for any firm, corporation or association of persons to hinder, limit or suspend the production or operation of utilities affecting the necessities of life, except upon application to and by the order of the Industrial Court.

Fifth, it declares it unlawful for any person, firm, corporation or association of persons to fail to or refuse to perform any act or duty enjoined by the provisions of the act, provided that nothing in the act shall restrict the rights of any individual employer or employee.

Sixth, it declares any person wilfully violating the provisions of the act guilty of a misdemeanor, and punishable by a fine not to exceed $1,000, or by imprisonment in the county jail for a period not exceeding one year, or both such fine and imprisonment.

Seventh, it declares that any officer of any firm or corporation engaged in any public utility industry, or any officer of a labor organization directly connected with any such industry, who shall wilfully use the authority of his official position to influence or compel any person to violate the provisions of the act, shall be deemed guilty of a felony and be punished by a fine not exceeding $5,000 or by imprisonment in the state penitentiary at hard labor for a term not exceeding two years or by both such fine and imprisonment.

The Kansas Court of Industrial Relations, in brief, was created to adjust labor differences in such industries as affect the necessities of life with the professed purpose of protecting the public interests involved; and furthermore it has been granted power to enforce its awards with a view to securing continuous operation of these same industries. In view of the important principle involved in this plan, a detailed account of the experiment is desirable.

The history of the legislation dates from the winter of 1919. The coal strike of that year, while it perhaps was not the sole cause of the legislation, tended greatly to make public opinion favorable to the plan. The coal miners of Kansas went on a strike for higher wages at the very time when the demand for coal was at its peak, and the resulting shortage caused the public, as well as the contending parties, to suffer great losses and hardship. Within two weeks after the beginning of the strike, many industries shut down, and many stores found it necessary to shorten their business hours for lack of fuel.

Governor Allen then issued a call for volunteers to operate the mines which were declared to be under the receivership of the State. The response was immediate, and within two days, more than eleven thousand men had been enlisted. Governor McKeley of Nebraska, declaring that his state was vitally affected by the strike, offered the services of fifteen hundred men in case they should be needed. A regiment of the Kansas National Guard was placed on duty at the mines. Six hundred men were detailed from General Wood's U. S. troops to form an encampment at the mines to cope with any emergency that might arise. When the volunteers arrived at Pittsburg, however, where trouble had been anticipated, there was no violence of any kind. The volunteers took possession of the mines and operated them without any disastrous interference from the union. Thus, the miners were defeated and forced to agree to resume operation of the mines. The result of this strike stimulated the enactment of the legislation.

The main features of the Kansas Plan were declared by William L. Huggins to have been first set forth in his speech at a Rotary Club luncheon, at Topeka, Kansas, October 30, 1919, under the title of "Is there a Labor Problem?" The speech commenced with a quotation from Kipling and a statement of the "most momentous problem" that was confronting the American people. A discussion of industrial organizations and their relations to the public followed. The trust was declared an illegal combination of corporations denying workmen the right of collective bargaining. Labor organizations were branded as constituting a "labor trust," dictating demands to the employers under the impending threat of a great strike, causing nation-wide suffering, and such action, in the words of Judge Huggins, should be denominated "'treason' and penalized accordingly." The speech continued with a proposal for an industrial code containing provisions for the administration of justice and the enforcement of its decrees. Under this code, various industries whose operation affects the living conditions of the general public would be required to place themselves under the supervision of the courts and a corresponding extension of the same principle would prevent organized labor from hindering, delaying or in any way restricting the operations of such industries. In conclusion, the proposal for an industrial code was reiterated with the assertion that the solution of the labor problem, or of any industrial problem, must be sought for and arrived at through legal formulas. In all matters of this nature, according to Judge Huggins, law is the panacea and law is supreme.

The actual planning of the Industrial Court, however, did not begin until January 5, 1920, while the State was still operating the mines. Governor Allen called the legislature in special session on this date for the purpose of enacting a law for the prevention of industrial warfare. At this time, the governor and some members of the legislature conducted a study of the arbitration laws and their results in different countries. They arrived at the conclusion that an industrial arbitration board, made up in the main of special pleaders and advocates of group interests, could scarcely be deemed an impartial and unprejudiced tribunal; and that industrial arbitration itself, placing emphasis as it does on the contending parties to the neglect of the public interest, could not be interpreted as an adequate system for settling labor disputes. The makers of the Kansas Industrial Court Act, therefore, turning their attention away from arbitration, thought that they could prevent industrial warfare by the enactment of a law making strikes, lockouts, boycotts and blacklists definitely unlawful.

The bill was prepared in a joint conference of the judiciary committees of both houses before its initial submission to the two branches of the legislature. When the bill was introduced in the House, it was decided to consider it in committee of the whole; the Senate, on the other hand, sent the bill to its judiciary committee for further consideration. The House held daily meetings to which senators were invited to submit their opinions, and in which representatives both of labor and capital were also given a hearing.[1] After some minor alterations which did not affect its general outline, the bill was passed 106 to 7 votes in the House, and 33 to 5 votes in the Senate. The law became effective January 24, 1920, and the Court was established on February 2, 1920, with William L. Huggins as presiding Judge.

The various arguments for and against the Court of Industrial Relations are of special interest and great importance.

[1] Senator Frank P. Walsh, J. I. Sheppard and Clarence Draper, Chairman of the Legislative Committee of the Mine Workers, spoke in behalf of the labor unions. Glen Willits, chairman of the joint legislative committee on labor, presided at all the meetings. William L. Huggins, Chairman of the Public Utilities Commission, made a speech in support of the bill. J. S. Dean followed, representing the mine operators. Addresses were made by William Allen White and Dr. E. J. Kulp, as representatives of the general public.

The main arguments in favor of the law are perhaps best presented by one of its originators, William L. Huggins, in his volume entitled *Labor and Democracy*. He approaches the subject with a general analysis of law and government, in the course of which he emphasizes as the two fundamentals of democracy: the rule of the majority and a government of law. Democracy, he maintains, means liberty of the individual, but this liberty must be limited by law, and no man can use his own in such a way as to injure his fellowmen. Judge Huggins frankly admits that judicial courts have not been entirely satisfactory, but they are proper and legitimate institutions, without which government cannot exist. "The government, registering the will of the majority, has by law provided for the peaceful and orderly adjudication of almost every possible human controversy except the industrial controversy." The prime purpose of the Kansas Act, it is here declared, is "to protect the public against the evils of industrial warfare." Judge Huggins' entire argument is based on three cardinal points: (1) the necessity of an industrial court to guarantee continuous operation of essential industries, (2) the duty of every citizen to show loyalty to the government, (3) and the guarantee of justice to labor by the enforcement of the Act.

1. It is asserted that modern economic conditions have made the manufacture of food and clothing and the production of fuel of tremendous and vital importance to the welfare of the public. The necessity for continuous operation of these industries in consequence is imperative. Section 6 of the Act declares: "It is necessary for the public peace, the public health and the general welfare that business shall be operated with reasonable continuity and efficiency in order that the people of this state

may live in peace and security and be supplied with the necessaries of life."

"We have created the Public Utilities Act," says Judge Huggins, "which compelled the railroads to run their trains . . . In this bill we are stepping out a bit further and saying that not only shall the electric light company be compelled to furnish service—and the water company—and the telephone company—but also because of the very necessities of the case, the people must also have food, clothing and fuel. Therefore we say to the concerns that furnish these necessities, 'you shall not cease operations and let the people freeze.'"

2. "Obedience to the law of the land," continues Judge Huggins, "is not debatable." Every patriotic citizen must make it his first duty to be loyal to the government. No good citizen will say that he owes his first duty to his own union or to his church. He owes his allegiance to the government.

3. Judge Huggins reached the kernel of his argument when he declared in a speech in defense of the bill before the Kansas legislature, that the act is "fair to labor." He goes on to explain what the bill has to offer to labor and how much it takes away from its prerogatives:

It offers a tribunal before which labor can go with any grievance which labor may have—that is labor in any of the industries described, and when labor approaches that tribunal, nobody can say, "Where is your bond for costs?" The poorest laborer in Kansas can walk into this tribunal with his pockets empty as the poorest man on earth and be heard. And further than that, as the matter proceeds, the State of Kansas provides that poor laborer with expert advice and expert assistance; it allows him to go wherever it may be necessary that he should go to take every bit of evidence that he wants to take without his employing an attorney, without

paying a dollar for traveling expenses or employing expert help of any kind.

Now is this an anti-strike bill? It certainly is not, and it is wrong to call it so. At least it is not an anti-strike bill in the sense in which they [its opponents] call it such. It does not prevent any man or set of men from leaving their work. It does say that when you quit, you quit. When you quit your employment you leave your job alone. And when you quit, if someone else wants to come and work in the place that you left you have no right to prevent him from doing it.

Judge Huggins, finally sums up his argument in the following statement: "And when you have given labor the better weapon, the court, and have given it the protection of law, you have the same right to take away the old weapon of the strike . . ."

The opposition to the law, on the other hand, is illustrated in the arguments of Senator Frank P. Walsh, in a speech delivered also before the Kansas legislature. Among Mr. Walsh's objections three points are of special significance: the unconstitutionality of the act, its dangerous tendency with respect to the fixation of rates and wages by the court, and the inevitable disastrous result of its attempt to destroy trade unionism.

1. The act is declared unconstitutional in that it violates the Thirteenth Amendment of the Federal Constitution, which provides that neither slavery nor involuntary servitude shall exist except in case of crime whereof the party shall have been duly convicted. Involuntary servitude is defined by the United States Supreme Court as "any control by which the personal service of a human being is disposed of or coerced for the benefit of another." Every possible freedom should be given to human ingenuity and human activity. Labor, finally, is not a commodity, and the human element should be first considered.

2. Mr. Walsh's second important charge is that the operation of the act will mean "state socialism in its most odious form." In Section 16 of the act, the government is empowered to fix rates, establish regulations, and control the operation of essential industries. While Mr. Walsh agrees that continuous operation of these industries is desirable, he strongly opposes the interference of the state in this matter.

3. The strongest objection from the standpoint of labor, is that the act deliberately aims to destroy trade unionism.

> Is it desirable to have labor unions? If it is, do not pass this law, because by passing it you strike down every labor union in the State of Kansas, and you draw a steel around your borders which says that labor unions cannot come in. The object that you give for Section 17 is a good object: that production shall not be hindered or delayed; that the public shall not be made to suffer on that account: and therefore certain things are made illegal. . . . No one would gainsay the right of the laborer to quit work or to say to his brother: "We are being imposed upon, we are not getting enough to eat, we are building up an immense fortune for this man, we do not ask much but we shall ask for a minimum wage." No man could object to that.

The most important arguments on each side have been sounded by Mr. Huggins and Mr. Walsh. To the one, law is supreme, and government of law is the highest form of civilization. To the other, liberty is a sacred human right without which there can be no true democracy, and in view of the deplorable suffering that labor undergoes daily, the strike, its only weapon in the struggle for existence, is too precious to forego. Other supporters and opponents of the law present almost identically the same arguments, approaching the subject perhaps from different angles, but reaching similar conclusions. Some more light may be thrown on the subject, however, by a consideration of the arguments of Samuel Gompers as contrasted to those of Governor Allen.

Mr. Gompers, in a debate with Governor Allen in Carnegie Hall, New York, May 28, 1920, makes two important points: the right of labor and relations between labor, capital, and the public. He declares that ownership and liberty are the two sacred rights of every free man.

> The free man's ownership of himself and his labor implies that he may sell it to another or withhold it; that he may, with others similarly situated, sell their labor power or withhold it; that no man has even an implied property right in the labor of another, that free men may sell their labor under stress of their needs, or they may withhold it to obtain more advantageous returns. Any legislation or court construction dealing with the subject of organizations, corporations, or trusts which curtail or corner the products of labor can have no true application to the association of free men in the disposition or withholding of their labor power.
>
> The attempt to deny free men by any process, the right of association, the right to withhold their labor power or to induce others to withhold their labor power . . . is an invasion of man's ownership of himself and of his labor power and is a claim of some form of property right in the workmen who have taken the places of strikers or men locked out.
>
> . . . It further follows that if free men avail themselves of the lawful right of withholding their labor power, they have the right to do all lawful things in pursuit of that lawful purpose. And neither courts, injunctions, nor any other processes have any proper application to deny to free men these lawful, constitutional, natural and inherent rights.[1]

[1] Allen, *The Party of the Third Part*, pp. 101–102.

Like Mr. Walsh, Mr. Gompers draws support from the Thirteenth Amendment to the Constitution of the United States, which provides that no man shall be forced into a form of involuntary servitude except as a punishment for crime. Mr. Gompers calls liberty the inalienable right of every free man, and it is unlawful for any man or organization to take that right from the working people.

Next, Mr. Gompers asserts that labor forms a considerable part of the general public, and that it is a common misconception of a large number of American people, and of the whole world, for that matter, to regard the interest of labor as opposed to that of the public. It is also a common error to consider the relative positions of labor and capital as exactly on an equal plane. Quite the contrary, labor represents the human effort, it is part of the man; while capital is merely the product of labor.

According to Mr. Gompers, the strike is a natural expression of unrest and as such is justifiable. The people of the United States undertake by voluntary negotiations between employers and employees to bring about agreements in the operation of industry. But when agreement fails, it means that circumstances do not permit the two parties to agree. It means that "the purchase and sale of labor power have proven unsatisfactory either to one or the other side, and each undertakes to do that which he has the lawful right to do—endeavor to persuade the other to his terms." So, in the opinion of Mr. Gompers, strikes are lawful and the right to strike must not be taken away. It is true that the public cannot afford to have a cessation of labor, but neither can the public afford to have degraded manhood.

Governor Allen, defending the law, also bases his

argument on two important counts: the legal justification of the act, and its beneficial aspects. The justification of the act is founded on the principle of government and police power. The functions of the police power are the protection of public health and public peace. Upon these foundations, the Industrial Court is built. Whenever strikes or lockouts threaten a shortage of the supply of necessaries, the government, for the interest of the public, may at once step in and interfere. The state does not wait until smallpox or yellow fever has invaded a community before taking action to prevent such contagious disease. It shuts up infected families within their dwellings, forfeiting temporarily their right to have direct contact with other members of the community. The same principle applies when a strike of considerable size endangers the public peace. The state has a perfect right to anticipate violence and provide measures to prevent it.

The beneficial aspects of the Industrial Court Act are enumerated by Governor Allen as follows: The Kansas law is not only concerned with the prevention of strikes so as to penalize labor, but it also forbids lockouts in the same industries; the law is fair to both employers and employees. "It proposes to curb the tyranny of capital just as stringently in its industrial relations as it curbs the tyranny of radical labor." The Court is given wide powers of investigation. It provides for publicity. It is given power to change regulations and practices, wages, hours, and working conditions. It entails no costs upon the penniless man who wishes to appeal to the court for justice. The law enters into the humanitarian phase of labor and provides for many preventive and constructive means of avoiding disputes. It has made careful studies of the cost of living and housing conditions in various industries, and such studies are beneficial to labor.

The clashes of opinion between the supporters of the law and its opponents are clearly and definitely marked. Governor Allen, like Mr. Huggins, maintains the law is constitutional. Mr. Gompers and his group say it is unconstitutional. Governor Allen states that individual liberty is a relative term and must be sacrificed for the good of the whole. Mr. Gompers vindicates liberty as the inalienable right of every free man, the sacrifice of which means nothing less than slavery. Whereas the constitution prohibits involuntary servitude. Governor Allen declares that the strike with all its evil consequences must be prohibited and prevented by law, making industrial warfare a criminal offense. Mr. Gompers maintains that the strike is a natural expression of disagreement between the man who has labor to sell and the man who wishes to buy labor; and that no law can compel a man to suffer continuously without resorting to an expression of his grievances. Take away the strike, and you will have the worst possible consequence—"the degradation of manhood."

The arguments of both sides are sincere. Governor Allen and his associates are right in the earnestness of their desire to protect public welfare. But neither are Mr. Gompers and his associates unreasonable in foreseeing that the consequence of such a law would be destruction of the whole labor movement, which means the perpetual subjugation of the working class to the rule of a few privileged groups.

One who considers the intricacies of the problem as a whole, however, must part company with Governor Allen and his associates. They are right in so far as the face value of their arguments is concerned. But they presuppose a number of important factors which tend to weaken their arguments on close examination. They presuppose, for example, the efficiency of the Court. They overlook the fact that the usual delays in the proceedings of a judicial court may be tolerated, but that any delay in the proceedings of the Industrial Court is unfair to labor. They fail again to appreciate the significance of the economic inequalities between the parties in a contention. The profit of a business concern is calculated according to its net earnings within a comparatively long period of time, for a firm may run at a loss in the first half year and yet make a huge profit at the end of the year by virtue of its increased earnings in the second half year. The earnings of a working man, however, cannot be considered in the same way. A wage-earner cannot live on a wage below the minimum of subsistence in one season and wait for a subsistence wage in the next. Likewise, he cannot continue his work in unsanitary or dangerous working conditions and wait for redress that may be granted in the coming year. A corporation is an artificial creature having neither flesh nor blood. On the contrary, the life of a human being is subject to the keen influences not only of physical and economic forces but of political and social forces as well. The human aspect of the problem, therefore, should receive the first consideration. In view of these circumstances, it is unfair to forfeit the workingman's right to strike and impose upon him equal responsibilities without giving due consideration to his financial inequalities.

Furthermore, the constitutionality of the Kansas Act is found wanting. Unless the provision of the Federal Constitution with respect to involuntary servitude should be amended, the Kansas Act is clearly a violation of that clause, and for this reason, it cannot be supported.

Finally, the legislation is inconsistent with the Fourteenth Amendment of the Constitution. Could the Government confiscate private property without due process of law? Could the Government fix wages and hours without infringing upon property rights? If the Fourteenth Amendment of the Constitution were to maintain legal competency, how could the Kansas Act harmonize itself with the due process clause? From the outset, therefore, the Industrial Court was not built upon firm foundations but upon sand, and when the storm came, it could not stand.

The storm did come, and the Kansas Court was swept away. The policies of the Court are now matters of history. The first severe blow dealt to the Act was the decision of the Supreme Court of the United States in the Wolff Packing Company case in 1922.[1] In this case the question of the validity of the Industrial Court was involved. By its decision in June, 1921, the Industrial Court raised the scale of wages of the employees of the packing company. The company refused to obey the order of the Court whereby the Court brought suit against the company. The State Supreme Court sustained the position of the Industrial Court and declared that "If the State can make regulations for the government of a business affected with a public interest, it ought to be able to extend the regulation to the wages paid to the employees of that business."[2]

The State Court argued further that laws fixing minimum wages and hours of labor for women were justified on moral and physical grounds, and laws fixing wages for men might also be justified on similar, although not the same, ground, "If the State under its police power

[1] 262 *U. S.*, 522 (1922).

[2] 109 *Kansas*, 646 (1921).

can interfere with that right [the right of contract for wages] on the part of women it ought to be, and is, able to interfere with the right on the part of a man." The State court frankly admitted that the Kansas Act creating the Court of Industrial Relations limited the freedom of contract: for "Practically every law regulating the conduct of men restrains their freedom of action, and practically every law regulating business affected with a public interest restricts the freedom of contract." But it denied that the order of the Industrial Court was an act in violation of the Fourteenth Amendment and that it deprived the defendant of his liberty and property without due process of law. The Court held that the defendant's business was one affected with a public interest, and that it ought to be subject to legislative control, but that the legislature which had taken that step to regulate in what manner the business should be conducted, "has not said that the defendant cannot under any circumstances cease to operate its packing plant if it desires to do so." Finally, the State Court upheld the order of the Industrial Court by citing the Wilson *vs.* New case[1] as a precedent. The Court pointed out the parallel circumstances which led to the enactment of the Adamson Law and the Industrial Court Act, and argued that since the Adamson Law was upheld by the Supreme Court of the United States, the Kansas Act of Industrial Relations was equally valid.

The company, however, carried the case to the Supreme Court of the United States. Chief Justice Taft, voicing the opinion of the Supreme Court, handed down a decision in favor of the plaintiff, the packing company. According to the Chief Justice, the case at hand could

[1] 243 *U. S.*, 332 (1916), ***infra***, p. 79.

not be considered subject to the jurisdiction of the public interest clause of the Kansas Act of Industrial Relations. The Industrial Act declares that the manufacture and preparation of food, the manufacture of clothing, the production of fuel and the transportation of the foregoing are all affected with a public interest. The Supreme Court, in contradiction, makes the distinction that the public interest is involved only in the case of *unusual circumstances* where there arises a particularly close relation between the public and those engaged in the industry. No general rule can be established applicable to the industries engaged in the manufacture or transportation of necessities of life and determining how far the Court may proceed in the fixing of wages. Public interest may be said to be involved either when, through the abuse of monopoly power, exorbitant prices are fixed, or when a strike or suspension of work curtails production, causing as a result great public inconvenience. But in the case under consideration, the Wolff Packing Company, being a small concern, its cessation of operation would not materially affect the meat and food supplies of the region. No monopoly exists in the packing industry in Kansas, no shortage of production; nor has there been any unreasonable advance in prices. Therefore, the particular circumstances which might have justified the Industrial Court in its action were declared not to exist in this case.

Moreover, according to the Chief Justice again, the contention that the fear of a strike in this particular establishment might spread to other similar establishments in the State, and thus curtail the food supply, was only a prophecy. The findings concerning the industry were prepared by a subordinate agency and its conclusions should not be taken so finally as to deprive individuals of their freedom of contract. The important question of whether the danger exists or not should be determined by the State legislature and not by the Industrial Court.

The Supreme Court declared further that in the matter of fixing rates and wages, rules and regulations, the Kansas Industrial Act "curtails the right of the employer, on the one hand, and of the employee, on the other, to contract about his affairs." Freedom of contract is held part of the liberty of the individual protected by the guarantee of the due-process clause of the Fourteenth Amendment.

While there is no such thing as absolute freedom of contract and it is subject to a variety of restraints, they [the restraints] must not be arbitrary or unreasonable. Freedom is a general rule, and restraint the exception. The legislative authority to abridge can be justified only by exceptional circumstances.

Chief Justice Taft concludes his decision by the declaration that the Industrial Court Act, in so far as it permits the fixing of wages in this case, is in conflict with the Fourteenth Amendment and deprives the firm of its property and liberty of contract without due process of law. Thus, the power of the Industrial Court was seriously limited and its future abolition became a question only of time and occasion.

The opposition of Governor J. M. Davis (Democrat), who succeeded Governor Allen (Republican), January 1, 1923, was another heavy blow to the Industrial Court. At the biennial legislative session in the spring of 1923, Governor Davis recommended that the Industrial Court Act be either repealed or modified. Failing to obtain a total repeal, the Governor suggested that the Court should consist of one judge together with two members of the public utilities commission to sit at hearings. The Republican majority of the session adopted a substitute measure for the Governor's recommendation, but then later killed its own proposal. The session came to an end with the Court barely escaping premature death.

Shortly after the decision of the Supreme Court in the Wolff Packing Company case, Governor Davis wrote to the three judges[1] requesting them to refrain from drawing their salaries and thereby voluntarily to abolish the Court. The Governor argued that the Supreme Court decision would seem to show that every power and duty of the Industrial Court, save those already covered in other statutes and imposed on other departments of the State Government, had been taken away. The judges did not follow the Governor's suggestion. The Court remained, but it was fighting a losing battle.

On March 10, 1925, the Court itself was abolished by Act of the legislature, which transferred all its powers and duties to the Public Service Commission.

A month after the legislature had abolished it, another case of the Wolff Packing Company was decided by the Supreme Court of the United States and that tribunal buried the Kansas Court. The dispute had to do this time with hours of work and working conditions. The Industrial Court, after it was denied power to fix wages, commanded the obedience of the packing company in the matter of a basic working day of eight hours to be observed in the packing industry, and a nine-hour day to be observed not to exceed two days in any

[1] The term of the former presiding judge, W. L. Huggins, having expired, Judge McDermott was appointed presiding judge in his stead, and Henderson S. Martin, a lawyer, was appointed to take the vacant place.

one week without penalty, provided that if the working hours of the week should exceed forty-eight in number, all overtime work should be paid for at a rate of time and a half, etc.

Justice van Deventer, who delivered the opinion of the Court, declared that the Kansas Court of Industrial Relations was built on the principle of compulsory arbitration. Under the Industrial Court Act, the disputant parties had no voice in selecting the agency to arbitrate or to investigate, and yet the award was binding on the parties "even to the point of preventing them from agreeing on any change in the terms fixed therein," unless the Court approved. Justice van Deventer held that the Supreme Court had pointed out before that the Kansas Act assumed as a "necessary postulate" that the State, in the interest of the public, "may compel those engaged in the manufacture of food and clothing, and the production of fuel, whether owners or workers, to continue in their business or employment on terms fixed by an agency of the State if they cannot agree." Furthermore, he denounced the system of compulsory arbitration as unconstitutional, when he said:

The system of compulsory arbitration which the Act establishes is intended to compel, and if sustained will compel, the owner and employees to continue the business on terms which are not of their making. It will constrain them not merely to respect the terms if they continue the business, but will constrain them to continue business on those terms. True, the terms have some qualifications, but as shown in the prior decision the qualifications are rather illusory and do not subtract much from the duty imposed. Such a system infringes the liberty of contract and rights of property guaranteed by the due process of law clause of the Fourteenth Amendment. "The established doctrine is that this liberty may not be interfered with under the guise of protecting the public interest, by legislative action which is arbitrary or without reasonable relation to some purpose within the competency of the State to effect." Meyer v. Nebraska, 262 U. S. 390, 399.

Finally, the Act was declared unconstitutional because it provided for the fixation of wages and hours of labor and was "merely a feature of the system of compulsory arbitration", and "as a part of the system, it shares the invalidity of the whole."

The Kansas plan belongs now to the past. The story of its romantic career has been completed. There is need, however, of some further explanation of the causes which brought about its death. There were no less than four obstacles which cut short its adventure.

1. Undoubtedly, the greatest of these causes is the objection to the principle upon which the Industrial Court was established. Compulsory arbitration, though it has been sometimes advocated by employers' associations and chambers of commerce, has not found general acceptance. The American Federation of Labor, as well as all other labor organizations, bitterly opposes the principle of arbitrary settlement. The American workers believe that the right to strike forms a large part of the right of their existence. Unless they can determine for themselves under what conditions, for how long and for how much they will sell their labor, they fear that the freedom of contract will be denied to them. The makers of the Industrial Court Act denied that the Court was founded on the principle of compulsory arbitration. Indeed there is a distinction between the Kansas plan and other systems of compulsory arbitration as they are in operation in Australasia. But so far as the principle of compulsion is concerned, the Kansas Court is not essentially different from other tribunals of similar nature.

2. The next cause of the failure of the Kansas Court was its wide jurisdiction without well-defined limits in regard to the application of the principle of public interest, which was not in harmony with the Federal Constitution. From the beginning the Kansas plan attempted to do too much. The Court was empowered to exercise police power and judicial as well as legislative and administrative powers. Let the question of the efficiency of the Court be taken for granted; the difficulty still remains. Inasmuch as the central argument for the Industrial Court rests on the principle of public interest, the problem is how far can this principle be made applicable to a given situation? In the Wolff case, for instance, the Industrial Court held that the packing company was engaged in the production of food, and therefore came under its jurisdiction. On the contrary, the Supreme Court of the United States unanimously declared that the given conditions of slaughtering cattle and packing meat were not sufficiently affected with a public interest. The existence of the Court, therefore, ultimately depended upon the judgment of the Supreme Justices.

3. Political influence certainly constitutes another great cause which, together with other forces, brought final destruction to the whole edifice of the Kansas Court of Industrial Relations. Ever since its establishment the Court had been a subject of controversy at successive elections and the center of other political manoeuvers. The judges of the Court were to be appointed by the Governor. The winning of the governorship by any organized group determined the kind of judges to be appointed and in turn the policy of the Court. The elections in Kansas during the Court's existence afforded no conclusive evidence as to how far political influences

would have served to bring about the Court's destruction. It was also true that some candidates for the legislature were elected on the issue of the Industrial Court, and others on this same issue were defeated. However, that the existence of the Court had been greatly imperiled by political changes cannot be denied. Governor Davis' opposition to the Court was a concrete example. Even Governor Allen himself, who formulated the plan, had entangled it in a political web. In 1921, he separated the function of the Public Utilities Commission from the Industrial Court and combined with the latter the functions of the labor department. Men who had served the Governor politically were appointed judges of the Court or members of the commission. No man who has read the first chapter of Governor Allen's book, *The Party of the Third Part*, can fail to realize that the dramatic narrative which the author so enthusiastically presents is saturated with the idea that the Industrial Court is a powerful vote-getting machine.

Judge Huggins, who opposes the mingling of the Industrial Court with other political machinery, has pointed out the danger of political influence on the judicial tribunal. He holds that the action of the Court should not be influenced by the probable effects on any political party. He makes a formal declaration of his stand when he says: "*If the Court of Industrial Relations cannot be kept free from the influence of politics and politicians, if it cannot be placed and kept upon the high plane of a judicial tribunal, it will fail and the law should be repealed before failure becomes disgrace.*" [1]

4. Finally, the last of the major causes of the collapse of the Industrial Court has been the instability of mob

[1] Huggins, *Labor and Democracy*, p. 89 (italics in original).

psychology. The law was passed after an act of emergency,—the government operation of the mines to break the coal strike. The volunteers were returned soldiers whose hearts were still burning with the fire of patriotism and whose sub-consciousness was still enslaved by the hysteria of war. The law was passed at a time when the legislature and executive officials temporarily and strangely forgot that they were human and fallible. The call of patriotism had immediate response from almost everywhere in the State of Kansas, and Governor Allen was the hero of the hour. But the Kansas Court has been incapable of standing the test of time. When the "mob" returned to their previous occupations, when Governor Allen ceased to make patriotic speeches, and when the public as well as the Supreme Court Justices had time to think the issue through, the Kansas Court of Industrial Relations could scarcely maintain its strong hold on the minds of men able to consider the problem in a scientific spirit.

CHAPTER III

Methods of Adjusting Railroad Labor Disputes in the United States

I. POSITIVE MEDIATION AND VOLUNTARY ARBITRATION—POLICY BEFORE 1914

The great strikes of 1877 marked the beginning of Federal intervention in railroad labor disputes in the United States. Never before had there been a time so alarming in the number and frequency of industrial strikes. From Baltimore to Chicago, from Boston to St. Louis, the whole country was shocked by the sudden outbreaks of violent industrial strife. The Governor of West Virginia appealed to the President for the assistance of the United States Militia to protect the people of that State. The Governor of Pennsylvania confessed his inability to suppress domestic violence and asked for Federal help. It was a time when President Hayes was called upon to order troops to the states. It was a time when the railroad companies tried every means to secure protection, while the workingmen held mass meetings to protest against the interference of Federal Militia. These great strikes were pictured as "a fool-hardy proceeding" causing violence and bloodshed.

As a result of this great upheaval in 1877, various States began to seek for means to prevent strikes by the enactment of arbitration laws.[1] But it was not until five

[1] Maryland, 1878; New Jersey, 1880; Pennsylvania, 1883; Ohio, 1885; New York, Massachusetts, Kansas, Iowa, 1886.

years later that the first resolution[1] was introduced into Congress calling for the appointment of a committee to investigate railroad labor disputes. Another resolution[2] was substituted for this one in the same year, requiring the committee to report on the causes of railroad labor controversies and the remedies for their adjustment. Various measures for railroad legislation were proposed in Congress in 1886. In 1887 the Interstate Commerce Act became law. One year later, Congress passed the Arbitration Act of 1888. Between 1888 and 1914 three statutes concerning railroad labor disputes were put in operation.

1. The Act of 1888[3] provided for the organization of a board of arbitration and a commission for investigation. It was enacted that whenever controversies arose between railroad companies and their employees, which differences might hinder transportation, upon the written proposal of either party to the controversy to submit their difference to arbitration, and upon the acceptance of the proposal by the other party, a board of arbitration should be created. The board should consist of three arbitrators, one to be elected by the employers, one to be elected by the employees, and the two should choose the third. All the arbitrators should be persons wholly impartial and disinterested in regard to the dispute. After the selection, the duty of the board was to organize at the place of origin of the controversy and to determine the matter of difference.

Together with the arbitration board, a temporary in-

[1] Introduced by Senator Morgan of Alabama, June 15, 1882, *Congressional Record*, vol. XIII, p. 4924.

[2] Introduced by Senator Blair of New Hampshire, June 28, 1882; *ibid.*, p. 5430.

[3] *United States Statutes at Large*, vol. 25, chap. 1063, pp. 501–504.

vestigation commission was to be created by the President. The commission for investigation should consist of three persons, the Commissioner of Labor and two persons appointed by the President, provided that one of these be selected from the State where the dispute occurred. The commissioners were to be directly responsible to the President and to render reports to the President and Congress. It is clear, therefore, that the main provisions of the Act were two, namely, for voluntary arbitration and government investigation.

With the exception of the investigation of the Pullman Strike of 1894, the Act remained a dead letter and never actually went into operation. This failure was due partly to the technical defects in the provisions of the law and partly to the fact that arbitration as a method of settling labor disputes was not well thought of at the time and consequently did not command the confidence of either party, the employers or employees. However, during this early period of railroad labor legislation, labor organizations generally aligned themselves in favor of arbitration. The Knights of Labor indorsed compulsory arbitration in the preamble to its constitution. Opposition to the law came chiefly from the employers.

The chief defect of this Act was that it had no provision for mediation and conciliation. Later records of labor disputes show that a majority of cases require no arbitration.

In spite of the apparent failure of the law, its significance should not be overlooked. This law marks the beginning of a new era in which government intervention in railroad labor disputes became established. Moreover, inasmuch as the law was the first of its kind, its makers can rightly claim that the success of later legislation has been made possible only as a result of their experiment.

2. The Erdman Act of 1898[1] corrected the defects of the Arbitration Act of 1888, by providing for mediation and conciliation as well as for arbitration. It provided that whenever differences threatening to interrupt railroad traffic arose between carriers and their employees, the Chairman of the Interstate Commerce Commission and the Commissioner of Labor should put themselves in communication with the parties to the controversy, and should use their best efforts by mediation and conciliation to arrive at a settlement. Only when such efforts were unsuccessful should the controversy be submitted to the arbitration of a board of three persons, and then only if arbitration were agreed to by both parties. The provisions for arbitration are as follows:

First, that the board of arbitration should consist of three persons,—one to be chosen by the employers, one by the employees and the two so chosen to select the third.

Second, that the board should find and file its award within thirty days of the date of appointment of the third arbitrator.

Third, that the award might be enforced in equity as far as the powers of a court of equity permit, provided no person should be compelled to the performance of labor against his own will.

Fourth, that dissatisfaction with the award gave no right to the employees to quit service nor to the employers to discharge any man until the expiration of three months from and after the making of the award; and then only upon the presentation of a thirty days' notice of such intention to quit or to discharge.

Fifth, that the award should continue in force for one

[1] *United States Statutes at Large*, vol. 30, chap. 370, pp. 424–428.

year, and no arbitration upon the same subject between the same parties should be had until the expiration of the time set forth.

Sixth, that during the pendency of arbitration, it should be unlawful for the employer to discharge the employees except for inefficiency, violation of law or neglect of duty; nor should it be lawful for the employees to strike.

Seventh, that violation of the Act should subject the offending party to liability for damage.

The main purpose of these provisions was to prevent strikes so as to guarantee continuous operation of the railroads. The attempt to realize this purpose was hastened by the Pullman strike of 1894 in which the Arbitration Act of 1888 failed to operate. The Erdman Act was a further step in the direction of government intervention in labor controversies.

While the railroad executives expressed doubts about the successful application of the Act,[1] Mr. Gompers, voicing the opinion of the American Federation of Labor, repeatedly testified that the Act was a piece of legislation destructive of the best interests of labor.[2] Commissioner of Labor Carroll D. Wright, advocating the settlement of labor disputes by arbitration, asserted that the legislation was in the right direction.

The first application of the law which occurred in 1899 proved a complete failure, as the following pages will show. After this failure, no attempt was made to use the law until seven years later in December, 1906. From that time on until the passage of the Newlands Act, July, 1913, sixty-one cases were adjusted under the Act. These cases, when classified according to the

[1] *The Railroad Gazette*, vol. XXX, May 13, 1898, p. 343.

[2] *American Federationist*, vol. III, February, 1897.

methods of adjustment, fall into three groups: twenty-six were adjusted by mediation, ten by mediation and arbitration, and six by arbitration alone.[1]

The frequent uses of the law at a later stage are to be explained by the fact that once mediation and arbitration had effected an amicable settlement, the result had a cumulative effect, and so the methods which brought about that result were demanded again. Applications for mediation were made not only by employees, but by employers as well. It was natural that when men thought that there was hope of adjusting differences, they would inevitably follow peaceful means rather than engage in struggles attended by suffering.

Yet in spite of the encouraging results, the law could not be called by any means a satisfactory measure. It fell short in four respects at least. First, the commissioners possessed no initiative power to act on their own motion. They could not render their services as mediators until one of the parties in the contention had applied for mediation and the other party accepted the invitation. Second, the arbitration board constituted of three persons proved inadequate. The decision eventually came to be controlled by the third arbitrator. Because of the tremendous power held by one person, it was difficult to secure a neutral arbitrator who would be satisfactory to both sides. Third, the temporary character of the board greatly limited the usefulness of the law. A new board was to be created for every new case. This meant great loss of time and efficiency. Finally, the rigid provisions for arbitration might also be called a defect, especially from the point of view of the labor organizations. The award of the arbitration board

[1] United States Bureau of Labor Statistics, *Bulletin* 303, p. 31.

bound the parties to a dispute for a period of one year; employees could not leave their employment until they had remained for three months after the award and had given a thirty days' notice of their intention so to quit. Indeed, employers were also bound by the same terms, but the difference in economic power makes a great difference in an equal sacrifice of opportunity. Mr. Gompers' objection to the Act probably rested on the same point, though he approached it from another angle when he made the statement that the Act was dangerous in the extreme in that it constituted "an attempt to wed the laborer to his employment."

The operation of the Act can best be demonstrated by a consideration of some of the important cases affecting the method of arbitration provided in the Act. The three outstanding cases, in this connection, are undoubtedly the Brotherhood of Railroad Trainmen's case of 1899, the Eastern Engineers' case of 1912, and the Eastern Firemen's case of 1913.

The Brotherhood of Railroad Trainmen's case of 1899 was the first attempt to utilize the Erdman law. A year after the passage of the law, an application filed by P. H. Morrissey, Grand Master of the Brotherhood of Railroad Trainmen, requested the Chairman of the Interstate Commerce Commission and the Commissioner of Labor to mediate in a controversy between the Brotherhood of Railroad Trainmen and seven railroads in the Pittsburgh district. The controversy had to do with wages and hours of the conductors and brakemen of these roads. The Board of Mediation accordingly communicated with the respective railroad managers on this matter, but the result was a flat refusal on their part.

The railroad managers argued that they could not increase the wages of the conductors and brakemen for various reasons. Among these reasons, two are worthy of note: first, that the increase of expenditure made for the improvement of tracks and equipment as a result of advances in the prices of material had already created a heavy burden on the roads; second, that the diminution of net receipts due to the decrease of transportation rates made it impossible for the management to consider any advance in the payroll.

But the underlying factor which led to the refusal of mediation in this case was not so much a question of the advance in wages as of the principle of arbitration which ultimately would affect the rights of the railroad managers in the fixing of the scale of wages. They feared that acceptance of the mediation of the Board would lead to arbitration, and they considered arbitration an infringement upon their rights. They sought to avoid government interference in the management of their affairs, and the mere acceptance of mediation would have opened the way for government intervention.

One railroad president,[1] expressing his objection to the provision of the Erdman Law for arbitration, said that the carrier while continuing to be responsible for the discharge of its duties to the public and to the stockholders thereby "abdicates its vital prerogative of determining what it can afford to pay its employees for their services, and transfers that prerogative to a special transcient committee of three arbitrators. . . ."[2] He gave as an expression of the opinion of the officers of his road that they could not in any manner relinquish to any tribunal but themselves their right of determining wages. He argued further that it was not "legally competent

[1] Bureau of Labor Statistics, *Bulletin*, No. 98, pp. 34-41.

[2] *Ibid.*, p. 36.

for them to permit the settlement of such a question by anybody other than by themselves acting in conjunction with their employees."[1] Another railroad executive of the Western District of Pennsylvania protested that the responsibility for the management of the property had been imposed upon him by the Circuit Court of the United States for the Western District of Pennsylvania, that it was therefore his duty to manage the property, but that he had "no authority to delegate the exercise of this responsibility to anyone else, either by way of mediation or arbitration. . . ."[2]

This case demonstrates concretely the attitude of the railroad executives toward government intervention in the period from the enactment of the law till 1906 when the Erdman Law was successfully utilized for the first time.[3] This attitude arose from a combination of fear and misunderstanding of the law. The meaning of the Erdman Law was not yet well appreciated, for the fairness of the law remained a doubtful question in the minds of the railroad officers. The fear and misunderstanding were, however, not entirely imaginary. The closing decade of the nineteenth century marked great steps in the direction of government intervention in the industrial field as a result of the enactment of the Sherman Anti-trust Law in 1890 and of the attempted proposals in Congress for strict governmental regulation

[1] *Op. cit.*, p. 37.

[2] *Ibid.*, p. 39.

[3] The locomotive firemen on the Southern Pacific Railroad on lines between New Orleans and El Paso, ordered a strike to become effective on December 23, 1906. A day before the strike became effective, the company invoked the Erdman Law and made application for mediation. The dispute was settled by arbitration in accordance with the law.

of big business. Managers of corporations were as keenly as ever on the lookout for signs of government interference and tried to avoid government intervention. Railroad executives were no exception to this rule.

Another important dispute was the Engineers' case of 1912. This case, involving the Brotherhood of Locomotive Engineers and the Eastern Railroads, presents a concrete example of the dissatisfaction toward the Erdman Law on the part of the railroad managements. The engineers asked for an increase of wages, for the application of the principle of standardization and for the exclusive right in the operation of the motive power regardless of the difference in the nature of power, whether it was steam or electricity. A conference between the representatives of the railroads and the men was held in New York. In this conference, Mr. Warren S. Stone, Grand Chief Engineer of the Brotherhood of Locomotive Engineers spoke for the Brotherhood. Mr. Stone defended the terms presented for consideration on the ground that the greater exertion required of the employees as a result of the increase in railroad traffic coupled with the increase in responsibility and discipline, justified the advance in wages. He held that with the introduction of larger locomotives, an engineer handled three times as much tonnage for the road as he handled previously and therefore deserved a higher wage than before as a proportional compensation for his service.[1] To this argument, Mr. J. C. Stuart, Vice-President of Erie Railroad and Chairman of the Conference Committee, replied that the use of larger locomotives was a part of the railroads' policy for economy and that the railroad

[1] *Conference on Wage Adjustment between the Eastern Railroads and the Brotherhood of Locomotive Engineers*, 1912, pp. 9 and 16.

operation should "be done sufficiently economically to be a going proposition, a business proposition."[1]

The next issue was the standardization of wages for engineers on all the Eastern railroads. This standardization did not imply uniformity of wages to all the engineers irrespective of their different classes. It meant that there should be a uniform rate on all the roads for the same class of engineers who performed practically identical tasks. The employees held that the variation of the financial ability to pay on the part of the roads should have no effect on this question. Furthermore, the engineers maintained that the conductors and trainmen of the same roads had already had uniformity in their wages; "Why can't we?" Mr. Stuart explained that from the management's point of view, the conductors and trainmen should not have had the uniform wages but that an unfortunate circumstance, a crisis, developed, and it seemed best for the interest of the public and all concerned to adopt that measure. Here the Chairman was apparently trapped, for Mr. Stone was stirred immediately to say, "Then the moral of that is, Mr. Stuart, we had better develop a crisis."[2] The Chairman attempted to defend himself by saying that he did not mean to convey that impression, but the fallacy of his logic seemed apparent.

As their last issue, the engineers demanded that they should have the exclusive right to run the electric engines in the event of a change from steam to electric engines. They held that it was unfair to them after working the best part of their lives on a road, to be dismissed when the road substituted electric transit for steam operation. The roads held that there was a great

[1] *Op. cit.*, p. 12.

[2] *Ibid.*, p. 26.

difference in the operation of the two systems and that the positions of the men should not be regarded as equal.

The Committee of Managers declined to grant any of the demands, and also refused to arbitrate. After this unsuccessful attempt, the Brotherhood of Locomotive Engineers took a strike vote, in which ninety-three per cent of the men were in favor of the strike. The gravity of this situation forced the roads to propose arbitration, but they succeeded in their refusal to arbitrate under the Erdman Act. They proposed a plan for arbitration under seven arbitrators, which was finally adopted. One arbitrator was to be selected from each party and the two so chosen were to choose the remaining five. In the event of a deadlock in the selection after fifteen days, the five arbitrators were to be selected by a committee consisting of the Chief Justice of the United States Supreme Court, the Judge of the Commerce Court, and the United States Commissioner of Labor. This expected deadlock did materialize. Consequently Chief Justice Edward D. White, Judge Martin A. Knapp and Commissioner Charles P. Neill were called upon to appoint the five arbitrators.[1]

The award of the board caused great dissatisfaction among the men. Wages were but slightly increased, the uniform rate was not granted and, with regard to transference to electric service, the engineers were given only the preference for the work but not the exclusive right. Moreover, the arbitration board made a recommendation signed by the majority of its members that there should be compulsory arbitration on the railroads. The great dissatisfaction of the engineers caused the firemen in

[1] The five arbitrators were: Hon. Oscar S. Straus of New York, Dr. Charles R. van Hise of Madison, Mr. Frederick N. Judson of St. Louis, Dr. Albert Shaw of New York and Mr. Otto M. Eidlitz of New York.

1913 on the same roads to stand firm in their refusal to arbitrate outside the Erdman Law.

The Firemen's case of 1913, which was the last important case under the Erdman Law, illustrates also the strong objections to the act on the part of the employers and their refusal to arbitrate under the act. It was only when the Brotherhood of Firemen and Enginemen flatly rejected the proposal of submitting the controversy to arbitration by agreement outside the law that the management yielded to the Brotherhood's demand to arbitrate under the act.

The principal issues at stake consisted of the demands for the uniformity of rates and rules, the increase of wages, the fixing of a day's work and the improvement of working conditions. The firemen demanded that rates of wages and rules of employment be made uniform on the railroads participating in the arbitration. The main reasons for this contention were that uniformity was necessary for adequate comparison of the existing scales of wage and rules with future conditions and changes,[1] and that the roads which could bear uniform cost of material, should be able to pay uniform wages.[2] The demand for the increase of wages would evaluate the scale of wages according to the weights of the locomotive. This was held to be a more accurate estimate of the value and proportion of the service of firemen, because the heavier and larger locomotive required greater energy for its operation. The contention for a ten-hour day was largely aimed at uniformity rather than shorter working hours, because thirty-eight of the fifty-four railroads affected had already inaugurated the ten-hour day

[1] *Arbitration between the Brotherhood of Locomotive Firemen and Enginemen and the Eastern Railroads*, 1913, p. 17.

[2] *Ibid.*, p. 19.

or its equivalent as estimated by mileage. The last of the main issues having reference to working conditions, demanded the employment of an additional fireman on locomotives weighing 200,000 pounds or more.

The significance of the case for the present treatise lies not so much in any justification of the demands as in the actual negotiations for arbitration on these demands. Upon the invitation to arbitration according to Federal law, the committee of managers of the roads suggested settlement on the basis of the engineers' award of 1912, and promised advances in the scale of wages, but rejected the demand for the additional employment of firemen on engines weighing 200,000 pounds. Mr. Elisha Lee, Chairman of the Committee of Managers writing in reply to Mr. Carter, President of the Brotherhood of Locomotive Firemen and Enginemen, said that the plan of arbitration should not exactly follow the lines of the Erdman Act, but that the number of arbitrators and the method of choosing them should be substantially the same as in the engineers' case.[1] The committee of managers raised another objection to the act, namely, that the time allowed for the arbitrators to render a decision was too short. The committee asserted that thirty days were not sufficient for the arbitrators to hear the full testimony and reach a satisfactory conclusion. On this objection, the employees agreed to extend the time from thirty days to sixty days, and suggested a further change in the agreement to arbitrate under the Erdman Law—that the right of appeal from the award to the Federal Court by either party to the controversy should be waived.

Summarizing their objections to arbitrate under the

[1] *Op. cit.*, p. 6.

Erdman Law, the committee of managers offered the following reasons: (1) that the responsibility which ultimately would rest upon the third member of the arbitration board was too great to impose upon one man; (2) that the ultimate decision of the third arbitrator would be a splitting of differences while the case might not be equitably adjusted without an adequate investigation; (3) that the public was not represented on the board of arbitration. The first two arguments were well founded, but the fallacy of the third objection appears conspicuously clear, as the third arbitrator did represent the public.

To these objections, Mr. Carter, voicing the opinion of the Brotherhood of Firemen and Enginemen, replied by rejecting the railroad's proposal, and in so doing, defended the Erdman Law. He maintained that after studying the engineers' case, the settlement of which was forced upon the employees, the firemen and enginemen had reached the conclusion that under no circumstance should they arbitrate according to the proposal of the railroads. He assailed the roads' methods of arbitration in that in the engineers' case only seven days were occupied with the submission of testimony, while six months were consumed before the publication of the award. His chief objections to the railroad plan were threefold:

(1) That the award might be based upon false evidence and thus it might do injustice to the employees.

(2) That while testimony and documentary evidence were of tremendous significance in the shaping of the award, the witnesses were not required to testify under oath and there was no legal machinery to penalize witnesses for false testimony.

(3) That in the case of arbitration under the railroads'

proposal, the employees were not given the chance to controvert false evidence after the closing of the hearing.

The inference to be drawn from Mr. Carter's arguments is that the Erdman Law was beneficial to the employees in that it provided for testimony under oath and made it possible to challenge fallacious evidence. This controversy between the firemen and the railroad management demonstrated the necessity for an amendment to the Erdman Law. For in this case, both parties were willing to submit their differences to arbitration, but both proposed different methods of adjustment. Both had the earnest desire to avert the unnecessary and destructive consequences of a strike, but each refused to submit to the proposal of the other. By a slight modification of the provisions of the law, both parties would be satisfied. To this end, the Newlands Act was materialized.

3. The Newlands Act made three important changes, namely, the creation of the "Board of Mediation and Conciliation", a new procedure of mediation and the selection of the number of arbitrators.

Under the Newlands Act, for the first time in the United States, an independent organization for the adjustment of labor disputes was created. This independent organization was the "Board of Mediation and Conciliation." The reason for the change was that railroad labor controversies had become extensive and continuous, and consequently, that it was difficult for a board as provided by the Erdman Act to function efficiently. The change in economic conditions required a modification of the law. Under the Erdman Act the Chairman of the Interstate Commerce Commission and the Commissioner of Labor constituted the board of mediation. But under the Newlands Act a board of three officials was to be appointed by the President, with the advice and consent of the Senate.[1]

The next change was in the procedure of mediation. Under the Erdman Act, the board of mediation could intervene only upon the fulfillment of two conditions: the application of one of the parties to a controversy for intervention, and the acceptance of the same by the other party. The Commissioner of Labor and the Chairman of the Interstate Commerce Commission were without authority to propose mediation. The Newlands Act, on the other hand, authorized "the Board of Mediation and Conciliation" to proffer its services to the parties in controversy, if in its judgment such action would be desirable. This clause, however, vested no power in the "Board of Mediation and Conciliation" to compel compliance with its intervention. It merely stated that the Board could offer its service, but the acceptance of such offer was entirely voluntary.

Another change occurred with regard to the members of the arbitration board and the time allowed for the choice of the third arbitrator. The parties to a controversy might submit their dispute to an arbitration board of three, or six members when they so preferred to stipulate. In the case of a board of three arbitrators each of the parties to the agreement to arbitration should name one arbitrator, and the two choose the third, and

[1] Mr. Seth Low, President of the National Civic Federation, Judge Martin A. Knapp, Chief Justice of the United States Commerce Court and Dr. Charles P. Neill, formerly Commissioner of Labor, strongly advocated this change. Judge Knapp and Dr. Neill were responsible for the operation of the Erdman Act, and this amendment was a result of their joint experiment. The successful operation of the Erdman Act, during the continuance of which only one unimportant railroad strike actually occurred, owed much to the efforts of Judge Knapp and Dr. Neill.

in case of failure of agreement with respect to the selection of the arbitrator within five days after their first meeting, the third arbitrator should be named by the Board of Mediation and Conciliation. But in the case of a board of six, each of the disputant parties should name two arbitrators and the four should select the remaining two, and fifteen days were to be allowed for the selection.

It has been observed already that the chief defect of the Erdman Law was the immense responsibility held by one arbitrator. The managers of the railroads refused to arbitrate under the law, as in the engineers' case of 1912 when they demanded arbitration under the sanction of mutual agreement among the parties themselves, for the reason that weighty financial questions and intricate details could not be handled satisfactorily by one man. In the firemen's case, the roads made a similar demand on the same ground. In the former case, the employees yielded to the demand of the roads, but in the latter, the employees insisted that their case be submitted to arbitration under the Erdman Law. It should be noted at this juncture that the insistence of the employees to submit their case to arbitration under the Erdman Law was not because they preferred to have three arbitrators, but because they, at this time, were still willing to entrust their fate to arbitrators and were not particularly concerned with the number of arbitrators, as long as they could effect a fair adjustment under the sanction of Federal law. Time and again they told the mediation board that it made no difference to them whether a board should consist of five or six or seven or any number of persons; they would accept any board that was provided by law.

The Newlands Act was invoked more frequently than the Erdman Act, for from June 30, 1913, to July 15, 1919, the Mediation Board adjusted 148 cases involving 586 railroads and 628,810 employees. This was due to the fact that at this period both employers and employees were willing to try arbitration in the adjustment of their differences.

The most important case which affected the method of arbitration was the controversy between the Western railroads and the Brotherhood of Locomotive Engineers and the Brotherhood of Locomotive Firemen and Enginemen of 1915. The result of this arbitration was entirely unsatisfactory to the men who protested against the selection of one of the neutral arbitrators. This arbitrator was Charles Nagel of St. Louis who had at one time been Secretary of Commerce and Labor. The ground for the vigorous protest, on the part of the men, against Mr. Nagel was that he had interest in some of the railroads involved in the dispute because he was a trustee of an estate owning some railroad bonds, the market value of which would be greatly affected by the arbitration award.

After this arbitration, the Brotherhoods publicly announced that they would not again enter into arbitration with the roads. Mr. Carter, President of the Locomotive Firemen and Enginemen, speaking before the Committee on Interstate and Foreign Commerce, said: "After years of experience under arbitration, I reached the conclusion: That the labor question is not arbitrable if the workingmen hope to secure justice in the results. . . . It is purely a class question, and these questions are not arbitrable."[1] Because of this attitude on the part of the Brotherhoods, coupled with the confidence in the strength of the concerted movement, the Brotherhoods refused arbitration in 1916, concerning the eight-hour-day controversy.

[1] *S. Doc. No. 549*, 64th Cong., 1st session, p. 143.

II. LEGISLATIVE SETTLEMENT AND WAGE BOARD ADJUSTMENT—POLICY DURING THE WORLD WAR

1. The Adamson Law[1] of 1916 is generally known as a law prescribing the eight-hour day. The law contained, however, essentially three provisions. First, eight hours should be deemed, in contracts for railroad labor and service, a day's work and the standard of a day's work for the purpose of reckoning the compensation for services of all employees to whom the act applies. Second, a commission of three, appointed by the President, was to investigate "the operation and effects of the institution of the eight-hour work day as above defined,"[2] and the facts and conditions effecting the relation between the roads and the men during a period of not less than six months or more than nine months from January 1, 1917. Finally, from January 1, 1917, until thirty days after the commission made its report, the existing standard day's wage should be the minimum wage for eight hours, and for every hour worked in excess of eight the men should receive at least one-eighth of the existing day's compensation.

The enactment of this law did not come as a result of deliberate planning by Congress, nor was it the fulfilment of a well defined policy of President Wilson. It was merely the effect of a grave emergency—the threat of the railroad Brotherhoods to call a general strike throughout the whole country. The passage of the law marked, however, a distinct departure in the policy pursued by the Government in its intervention in labor disputes. In fact, this episode in which the labor or-

[1] *United States Statutes at Large*, vol. 39, chap. 436.

[2] *Ibid.*, sec. 2.

ganizations successfully threatened the Government with a general strike, finds no parallel in the entire history of the United States, and it is the only case in which the Government has settled a labor dispute by legislative enactment.

The significance of the Act rests not so much on its provisions as on the gravity of the situation which caused the Act to be hurried through Congress. The legislation for an eight-hour day is no longer a radical measure. But the way in which the Brotherhoods demonstrated their organized strength and the response of the Government in legislating to avert the strike, created a situation which is of greater significance than the provisions of the law.

The history of the controversy, which led up to the legislation, began in a demand of the Four Brotherhoods[1] in December, 1915. The committee representing the Brotherhoods at a meeting in Chicago formulated the propositions that the payment of wages should be based on an eight-hour day for on mileage of 12½ miles as the equivalent of an hour, and that time and one-half should be paid for overtime.

In January, 1916, the Executive Committee of the Association of Western Railroads issued statements criticising and counteracting the Brotherhood's demands.[2] It was pointed out that the employees' proposal was not one for an eight-hour day but only for the increase of wages of 25 per cent after an increase had been made by the board of arbitration a few months before. The com-

[1] The four Brotherhoods are, namely, the Brotherhood of Locomotive Engineers, the Brotherhood of Locomotive Firemen and Enginemen, the Brotherhood of Railway Conductors and the Brotherhood of Railroad Trainmen.

[2] *Railway Age Gazette*, 1916, vol. 60, No. 3, p. 206.

mittee criticised the latter part of the proposal for time and one-half by means of the argument that the Brotherhoods failed to take into consideration the difference in the nature of the work between the railroad service and work in other industries. The committee maintained that in other industries the employers could control the amount of overtime while it was beyond the power of the railroad management to do the same. The argument for the roads was reenforced by S. W. Thompson, Vice-President of the Baltimore and Ohio Railroad.[1] The position of the roads was defended on technical ground, that the income of the roads was regulated by law, for it depended upon the judgment of the Interstate Commerce Commission. On the other hand, there was no provision requiring the commission to fix the amount of the railroad earnings devoted to the payment of wages.

The negotiations for the eight-hour day went on. On March 30 of the same year a formal proposal to the roads was made.[2] On the same day, the Executive Committee of the Western Railroad Association issued its counter proposal explaining the position of the Western railroads.[3] On April 25, the directors of the Chamber of Commerce of the United States ordered a referendum to be taken on a proposal "to ask Congress to call upon the Interstate Commerce Commission to investigate at once all the facts bearing on the demands of railroad employees for increased pay."[4] On April 27, the first conference was held between the executive sec-

[1] In an address before the Pittsburgh Chamber of Commerce, on March 14, 1916, *op. cit.*, No. 13, pp. 762-3.

[2] *Railway Age Gazette*, May 5, 1916, p. 1005.

[3] *Ibid.*, April 7, 1915, p. 785.

[4] *Ibid.*, p. 964.

retaries of the conference committees of managers of Eastern and Western Railroads and the Presidents of the Four Brotherhoods. In this conference, it was "practically decided" to begin a formal conference between the representatives of both parties in New York City on June 1; and on that date, the representatives did actually begin formal negotiations. Their daily discussions, however, were fruitless. After two weeks of haggling over terms, the managers proposed that the matter be submitted to the Interstate Commerce Commission for settlement or to arbitration under the Newlands Act. This proposal, the employees rejected. Mr. Garreston, President of the Order of Railway Conductors, voicing the opinion of the employees, said that their experience had shown that arbitration had driven a large proportion of their membership into an attitude of opposition to arbitration largely because of "the inability to secure neutral arbitrators who were able to grasp the intricacies of the question."[1]

The gravity of the situation continued to develop. In the last week of June, the railroads conducted a nation-wide advertising campaign through the press setting forth arguments in defense of their position and advocating their methods of adjustment by arbitration.[2] The Brotherhoods in defending their position stated that in spite of the tremendous efforts which had been spent in negotiation, the managers' committee made no definite offer. The Brotherhoods maintained that they rejected the proposition for submitting the case to the Interstate Commerce Commission because in their opinion the Commission had no authority under law to regulate

[1] *Op. cit.*, 1916, p. 1536.

[2] *Ibid.*, p. 1587 (1916).

wages. In fact they objected to the principles of arbitration entirely. They asserted that the roads had no more right to insist on arbitration to force their employees to work excessive hours and to receive wages fixed by a commission than to fix the prices at which dealers of railroad supplies should sell their goods.[1] Conferences between the parties were held in August, but each side maintained its position unchanged.

Upon the failure of both sides to reach an agreement, the Brotherhoods voted to order a strike on the fourth of September. This led to the intervention of President Wilson, who proposed arbitration. The employers agreed to it, but the Brotherhoods rejected it. The President then urged that both sides should accept the eight-hour day on the existing basis of pay and that the question of pay for overtime be submitted to a commission authorized by Congress. While the Brotherhoods accepted the proposition, the roads refused to comply and insisted on arbitration. This unexpected failure in mediation coupled with an earnest desire to avert the strike, led the President to appeal to Congress for the enactment of an eight-hour-day law for the railway employees. The Adamson law was then hastily passed, although the justification for this enactment caused heated debates in Congress.

Representative Adamson explained that there was nothing dangerous in enacting an eight-hour-day law for the railroads, asserting that the question of the eight-hour day was not a new one, and that the seriousness of the matter was in the situation confronting the country at large.[2] Representative Caldwell from New

[1] *The Railway Conductor*, 1916, p. 531.

[2] *Congressional Record*, 1916, p. 13584.

York voiced the opinion that eight hours were long enough for any man to work in a skilled trade and that the adoption of the eight-hour day was a great step in advance toward the realization of a democratic principle.[1]

Strong opposition was raised by the Republican members of the House. The opinion of Representative Bennet of New York, in this respect, was the most prominent. He declared that the passage of the Act was worse than a strike. It indicated "the destruction of the American system of government." Moreover, the proposed legislation was "the worst blow that anyone ever dealt at organized labor." The action was characterized as an act compelling Congress to pass the law within a certain time regardless of whether that legislation was legal or illegal. "I for one do not propose . . . to cast my vote with a pistol against my head." Mr. Bennet went on to denounce the bill on constitutional and practical grounds. He called it unconstitutional to compel the roads to pay ten hours wages for eight hours service. He denounced the Act as revolutionary and impracticable in that the fixing of railroad wages implied the regulation of wages of all other industries. He declared that when the government came to regulate the rate of wages, the sheer weight of labor would render the function of the government ineffective.

However, the majority of both Houses felt the situation justified the legislation. Furthermore, they believed that Congress had the power to regulate interstate commerce, and since this controversy was a matter affecting interstate commerce, Congress had the power to enact measures for the prevention of a public calamity.

[1] *Op. cit.*, p. 13582.

[2] *Ibid.*, p. 13579.

The constitutionality of the act was upheld by the Supreme Court in the case of Wilson *v.* New.[1] Chief Justice White, who delivered the opinion of the Court, asserted that the business of common carriers by rail is in a sense a public business, and that public interest begets a public right of regulation. Furthermore, the imminent situation which endangered public welfare warranted the legislation at this time. If there were no power to remedy a grave situation resulting from dispute between employers and employees, the public would be left helpless. The power of Congress to regulate "embraces the right to control the contract power of the carrier in so far as public interest requires such limitations. . . ."

More important yet, Chief Justice White declared that Congress had the power even to provide for compulsory arbitration for railroad labor disputes. This decision was certainly a great step forward in the direction of positive governmental intervention in industrial controversies.

2. Wage-board adjustment was the machinery used during the War.

When the United States entered the War, the country faced a huge augmentation in the demand for food and war supplies. The production program became unprecedented. But unless uninterrupted transportation could be guaranteed, troops and munitions would be made helplessly idle, business and industries would be crippled and the consequence for the community would be disastrous. Therefore, soon after the proclamation of war, the Federal Control Act[2] was passed empowering the

[1] 243 *U. S.*, 332 (1916).

[2] The Act was signed by President Wilson on March 21, 1918.

Government to operate the railroads and creating the position of Director General of Railroads in order to centralize the operation and control of the roads and to deal more effectively with the employees. For the prevention of any cessation of work on the railroads, machinery was provided for the adjustment of differences between employees and management.

During the war two commissions were created to adjust railroad labor differences: the Railroad Wage Commission and the Board of Railroad Wage and Working Conditions. The purpose of the Wage Commission was in the main to make an investigation of the railroad wages and their relationship to the cost of living and to the wages paid in other industries. The Wage Commission was to report its findings to the Railroad Director General, and after its report, it automatically went out of existence. When the Commission began its investigation it was confronted by the colossal task of adjusting many varieties of wage-scales established by more than one hundred and fifty roads, and involving more than two million employees. After a three months' careful consideration, the Commission finally took the increase in the cost of living from December, 1915, as the basis for determining the flat increases in wages, which it recommended.

After the Wage Commission had gone out of existence, the Board of Wages and Working Conditions took its place. The Board was "solely an advisory body." It submitted its findings to the Director-General, who ordered such measures as he approved. The duty of the Board was essentially to investigate all questions concerning wages and working conditions.

For the purpose of settling labor disputes, three adjustment boards were created, known as Boards of

Adjustment Nos. 1, 2 and 3. Board of Adjustment No. 1 dealt with disputes involving the men connected with the movement of trains; No. 2 dealt with the railway workers in shops and with the carmen; No. 3 handled the employees in the maintenance of way division, switchmen, telegraph operators, etc. In spite of prevailing opinion that a bipartisan board would deadlock, the employers and employees had equal representation on these boards, and their decisions were invariably unanimous. These three boards, from the dates of their formation[1] to January, 1920, settled over 3100 controversies without a dissenting vote and without a single deadlock.

After the termination of the Great War, President Wilson in 1919 called an industrial conference composed of representatives of employers, employees and the public. But this conference was fruitless. A Second Industrial Conference was called in December of the same year. It was composed of representatives of the public only. The second conference proposed a plan for joint organization, representing management and employees, as an effective means of preventing disputes.[2] It offered also a plan for the adjustment of disputes.

The machinery for adjustment consisted of a national industrial board and local regional conferences and boards of inquiry. The United States was to be divided into regional sections with a regional board responsible for each section. The regional board should consist of nine members, including the chairman, who should be a government official. The other members of the board were to be selected by the parties themselves, but four

[1] Adjustment Board No. 1 was organized April 8, 1918; Board No. 2 on May 31, 1918; Board No. 3, August 18, 1918.

[2] Report of President's Industrial Conference, January, 1920.

of them must be chosen from the industry concerned. When unanimous agreement in the regional board failed, the matter then should be referred to the national industrial board. This national tribunal, having its headquarters in Washington, also should consist of nine members, three representatives from employers, three from employees, and three from the public, all appointed by the President, and their appointments confirmed by the Senate. While the decision of this National agency, according to the plan, should be final, no legal penalty should be imposed in case of refusal to abide by its determination. A regional board of inquiry was to be created only when there was no voluntary submission of a dispute to the regional adjustment board.

This was an intricate plan carefully formulated for the adjustment of labor differences under American conditions. Unfortunately, the conflicting interests of employers and labor organizations prevented its adoption at the time, although some of the provisions of this plan are found in the Transportation Act. The purpose of the conference, however, was not primarily for setting up machinery for the adjustment of railroad labor disputes alone, but had the recommendations of the conference been adopted, the railroads would have been greatly concerned with the legislation.

III. ADVISORY DETERMINATION—POLICY SINCE 1920

The events which led to the enactment of the Esch-Cummins law date back to the Federal Control Act of March 21, 1918. The Federal Control Act provided for the Federal operation of the properties of the carriers during the war and for a reasonable time thereafter. Consequently, when the war ended in 1919, it was necessary for the Federal Government to return the roads to their original owners. On March 1, 1920, the Government relinquished its control and operation of the railroads in accordance with the provisions of the Transportation Act.

The Transportation Act was the result of a merging of two separate bills: the Cummins Bill which was passed by the Senate, and the Esch Bill which was passed by the House. After heated debates and careful consideration by both Houses, a combination of these two measures was worked out as a compromise.

The Act consists of five titles. The first two titles deal with definitions and the termination of Federal control. The last two titles contain the amendments to the Interstate Commerce Act and other miscellaneous provisions. The third tittle contains the labor provisions, with which this chapter is concerned.[1]

Basing their work on the success and failure of previous statutes, the originators of the Esch-Cummins Act emphasize mediation and conciliation. In Section 301 of the Act, it is provided that all disputes between carriers and employees shall be considered and, if possible, decided in conference between representatives of both parties. In case any dispute, except one involving wages, is not decided in such conference, it shall be referred by the parties to the Railroad Board of Labor Adjustment.

An adjustment board may be organized "by agreement between any carrier, group of carriers or carrier as a whole, any employees or subordinate officials of carriers or organization or a group of organizations

[1] The Transportation Act contains no provision calling for the repeal of the Newlands Act. The United States Board of Mediation and Conciliation, created by the Newlands Act was abolished, however, on December 1, 1921.

thereof." There are four possible ways by which a dispute may be referred to an adjustment board.

1. Upon the application of the chief executive of any carrier or organization of employees or subordinate officials whose members are directly interested in the dispute.

2. Upon the written petition signed by not less than 100 unorganized employees or subordinate officials directly interested in the dispute.

3. Upon the adjustment board's own motion.

4. Upon the request of the Labor Board whenever the Board is of the opinion that the dispute is likely substantially to interrupt commerce.

The most important section among the labor provisions of the Transportation Act is the provision for the establishment of the Railroad Labor Board, which is composed of nine members: three members representing labor, three members representing management and the remaining three representing the public. The labor and the management representatives are appointed by the President, by and with the consent of the Senate, from not less than six nominees from each of the respective groups, the nominations being made by the parties themselves. The neutral members are appointed directly by the President, by and with the advice and consent of the Senate. All wage disputes go directly to the Board, and under the following circumstances, the Board hears and decides all matters involving grievances over wages as well as working conditions:

1. Upon an adjustment board's own motion to certify to the Labor Board that the Adjustment Board has failed to reach a decision within a reasonable time.

2. When, according to the opinion of the Labor

Board, "the Adjustment Board has so failed or is not using due diligence in the consideration."

3. When an adjustment board has not been organized, upon the application of the chief executive of any carrier or organization of employees, or subordinate officials whose members are directly interested in the dispute, or upon a petition signed by not less than 100 unorganized employees or subordinate officials directly interested in the dispute, or upon the Labor Board's own motion.

The decisions of the Labor Board have two important aspects: in the first place, they are final, though the operation of the decision may be suspended within ten days if the Labor Board is of the opinion that the decision will involve a readjustment of rates. Such suspension is possible, however, only when at least one representative of the public shall concur to act in its favor. In the second place, the award of the Labor Board is only advisory. The Board is not empowered to enforce its decision, though when it has reason to believe that any of its own decisions, or any of those of an adjustment board, is being violated by a carrier or employee or organization thereof, "it may upon its own motion after due notice and hearing to all persons directly interested in such violation, determine whether in its opinion such violation has occurred and make public its decision in such manner as it may determine."

In determining what is a just and reasonable wage, the Board is required to take into consideration, among other relevant circumstances:

(1) The scales of wages paid for similar kinds of work in other industries;
(2) The relation between wages and the cost of living;
(3) The hazards of the employment;

(4) The training and skill required;
(5) The degree of responsibility;
(6) The character and regularity of the employment, and
(7) Inequalities of increases in wages or of treatment, the result of previous wage orders or adjustments.

The passage of the Act caused heated discussions throughout the country. The labor organizations were strongly against the passage of the Bill. When it was pending for decision in Congress, they did what they could to prevent its passage. When the Bill reached the President, they tried to persuade him to withhold his signature. The resolution unanimously adopted by the "Standard Recognized Railroad Organizations" shows the strong opposition of the railroad workers to the Bill:

. . . Whereas the provisions of the bill creating the Labor Board permit indefinite delays in the creation of the Board. . . .

Whereas the provisions of the Bill abrogate the right of collective bargaining and substitute therefor an indefinite and uncertain method of compulsory adjustment or arbitration of disputes, now, therefore,

Be it resolved, that we, the organized body of employees, making possible the operation of the railway systems of the United States, . . . with a full sense of responsibility to ourselves, do now request that you veto this bill and return it to the Congress of the United States without your approval, firmly believing that only by such course can an orderly solution of the problem now confronting the American people be achieved.[1]

Looking at the opposite camp, different points of view are in evidence. While the railroad executives regarded the Act as an experiment, they considered it as about as good a measure as could be expected from Con-

[1] *The Railway Telegrapher*, March, 1920, pp. 308-310.

gress. At any rate, a compromise, though it might greatly injure the constructive character of the legislation, was still better than government control. Just before the termination of Federal Control, the Association of Railroad Executives, after a formal meeting, made public a declaration which contained the following statement:

> The Act itself is about to enter upon its test period. If under the system which it establishes, the credit of the carriers is made sufficient to enable them to perform their public duties, the legislation will, by universal concession, be a success. If, on the other hand, such credit is not established, the legislation will be a failure.[1]

In the opinion of President Wilson, the bill safeguarded the just interests of railroad labor. In spite of the strong demands from the labor organizations, petitioning him to exercise his power to veto the bill, he affixed his signature, and the bill became a law. In a letter addressed to the Railroad Brotherhoods, as a reply to their request that he should veto the bill, he fully expressed his opinion concerning the Act. The leading points of the letter were:

> The bill having now become a law, the way is open for immediate action on the wage matter in accordance with the terms of the bill. . . .
>
> The argument that the public representatives on the Labor Board will be prejudiced against labor, because drawn from classes of society antagonistic to labor, can and ought to be overcome by selecting such public representatives as cannot

[1] The meeting was presided over by Thomas De Witt Cuyler, Chairman of the Association. The statement was prepared for the press by Alfred E. Thom, General Counsel. *New York Times*, February 28, 1920.

be charged with any such prejudices. Nor do I anticipate that the public representatives will be against wage increases. Not only must public representatives be selected who can be relied upon to do justice, but the bill itself provides that the labor board shall establish rates and wages and salaries which, in the opinion of the board, are "just and reasonable", and it is further provided that the entire labor board shall be guided by the very important standards which are provided in the law. . . .

My hopes are that the putting into effect of these provisions, with a carefully selected labor board, whose public representatives can be relied upon to be fair to labor and to appreciate the point of view of labor that it is no longer to be considered as a mere commodity, will mark the beginning of a new era of better understanding between the railroad managements and their employees, and will furnish additional safeguards to the just interests of railroad labor. . . .

The Railroad Labor Board was organized on April 16, 1920, and it has been functioning since. The first task of the Labor Board was to attempt an occupational classification of railroad positions. The purpose of this classification was to obtain a basis for describing the classes of position so as to secure an adequate terminology. Without such classification, the Board would be helpless when it comes to rendering its decisions.

The interpretation of the Transportation Act remains one of the great tasks confronting the Board. The adjustment of wages according to the cost of living has been the storm center of many a violent debate among the members of the Board. The labor representatives hold it to have meant one thing and the representatives of the employers maintain it to have meant another.

This aspect of the work of the Railroad Labor Board can best be illustrated by considering some of the

Board's decisions. Take for example, Decision No. 1267, the case of the United States Brotherhood of Maintenance of Way employees and Railway Shop Laborers *et al. v.* Alabama and Vicksburg Railway Company *et al.*, October 16, 1922. There were one hundred and twenty-one railroad companies involved in the dispute. This case is of great interest, because it developed out of a series of controversies, which reveal the difficulties with which the Labor Board has to deal.

The history of the case goes back to the first decision of the Board in dealing with wage matters. By its decision No. 2 (1920), the Labor Board granted increases in the wages per hour for the Maintenance of Way and Shop employees. But by its decision No. 147, effective on July 1, 1921, it reduced the wages per hour of this class of employees. Again, by its decision No. 1028, effective July 1, 1922, the Labor Board further reduced the wages per hour of this class of employees. But by its decision No. 1267, effective October 16, 1922, the Board slightly increased the wages per hour of some of the groups of the Maintenance of Way and Shop laborers.

The Labor Board supported its decisions on the ground that they were based on the seven elements for determining a just and reasonable wage, as provided in the Transportation Act. The Board explained in decision No. 1028, that after the reductions made under that decision, common laborers on the railroads would still receive wages in excess of those paid to similar classes of labor in other industries, and that the same is true of all other classes of labor governed by that decision. It further declared that according to the report of the United States Department of Labor, the cost of living had decreased since 1920, and that the reductions were justified in consequence. In its decision No. 1267, the Board argued that since there had been no pronounced change in the cost of living since March, 1922, a conservative increase of wages was just and reasonable.

In their dissenting opinion from the majority opinion of Decision No. 1267, the labor members of the Board present different arguments:

1. That in spite of the fact that the wages paid to railroad laborers are on a higher level than those paid by private industries, "this does not alter the fundamental mandate of the law that wages shall be just and reasonable. The relation of rates of pay to those established in private industries, or the relation of rate of pay to the cost of living, is a secondary consideration which does not come into play until the primary requirement of a just, a reasonable, or an adequate, or living, wage has been satisfied."

2. That the living wage is legally sound. It is the duty of the Board to accept and apply it. "The former National War Labor Board had adopted the principle that 'the right of all workers including common laborers, to a living wage is hereby declared.'".

3. That "the budgetary method is necessary and practicable. A budget must be constructed to cover the quantities of food-stuffs and clothing which an average family requires in order to be properly nourished and decently clothed, necessary housing facilities and fuel, and sundries or miscellaneous articles essential to modest and frugal comfort."

To these arguments, the majority of the Board reply in their supporting opinion that the fundamentul difference between the supporting opinion and the dissenting opinion is that the former is based on the provisions of the Transportation Act and the latter is based on an idealistic theory of what ought to be. They declare that the duty of the Board is to give due weight to the seven factors enumerated in the Transportation Act.[1]

The conflict of opinion with respect to the interpretation of the law and the limitations and inadequacy of the Act itself, are indicative of the difficulties and obstacles which the Labor Board has to face. It is a defect of the capitalistic order that the adjustment of wages depends so much upon the ups and downs of industry and the rise and fall of the cost of living, Yet, under the circumstances, the method of advisory determination is the best the Government can inaugurate in order that employers and employees may arrive at some point of satisfactory agreement.

Moreover, even when the cost of living is accepted as the essential basis for wage adjustment, much difficulty still remains. What kind of statistics should be used? How large is an average family? How can a workingman's budget be determined? Each of these questions presents a complicated problem in itself. Should the Board conduct a separate investigation and form its own statistics, or should it accept the findings of other institutions? The Board, in rendering its decisions, must have accurate data at its command supported by genuine facts. There will be no agreement when both parties to a dispute twist facts to suit their purposes. No matter what the subject of dispute may be, the actual facts concerning the industry must be accurately known and the disputants must agree on this point. It is a deplorable situation that the most important disputes which the Labor Board has dealt with, have been, in essence, controversies over the interpretation of actual facts.

[1] *U. S. Railroad Labor Board Decision*, 1922, No. 1267, pp. 20-36.

The controversy between the Pennsylvania Railroad and its employees on the question of proper representatives reveals another aspect of the work of the Labor Board. This controversy throws light on the authority and legality of the rulings of the Board. It consisted of two similar disputes, namely, (1) the Railway Employees' Department of the A. F. of L. (Federal Shop Crafts) *v.* Pennsylvania System; (2) the Brotherhood of Railway and Steamship Clerks, Freight Handlers, Express and Station Employees *v.* Pennsylvania System.[1] In both cases the question of the procedure and methods of electing representatives for the employees was involved.

In the former case, the representatives of the carrier met the officers of the labor organization (System Federation No. 90), but refused to negotiate with them on the ground that "there was not satisfactory proof that the system federation actually represented the employees in question." In order to secure satisfactory evidence on this point, the representatives of the road announced their plan to conduct a secret ballot among the shop-craft employees. To this plan, the officers of the System Federation No. 90 objected, but proposed that the ballot, if it were to be conducted, should allow the voters to vote for an organization, if they desired. The management declined this proposal and conducted a ballot as originally proposed. At the same time, the union conducted a ballot for its members and declared that the company's ballot was illegal. As a result, out of the 33,104 men in the Altoona shops, only 3,480 voted and the rest or 89.5 per cent were virtually disfranchised.[2]

[1] *Railroad Labor Board Decisions* (1921), Nos. 218 and 220 respectively.

[2] The figures were presented to the Labor Board by the management. The union did not disclose the result of its ballot. *Ibid.*, p. 211.

The union contended that the fact showed conclusively that the shop-crafts did not vote for the representatives whom the company recognized. To this the company replied that it was immaterial whether the majority of the employees voted or not and that the company should deal with the representatives elected by the majority of those who did vote.

In the latter case, the Pennsylvania railroad put out a ballot to the railway and steamship clerks, freight handlers and proceeded to deal with representatives thus elected by the minority of the employees according to the company's plan. This plan provided that negotiation between employer and employees should be carried on in separate territorial divisions rather than with the class of employees as a whole.

Both cases were brought before the Railroad Labor Board, and in each case the employees presented practically identical arguments in protesting the injustice done by the management. Their first objection was that the election conducted in accordance with the company's plan did not permit the employees to vote for an organization, but limited their rights to elect individuals only. In the second place the carrier's plan required the individuals so chosen to be employees of the company. Lastly, the carrier had arbitrarily divided the employees of the class into subdivisions without their consent. The Labor Board after examining the evidence advanced declared the elections illegal and ordered the company to conduct a new election according to the advice of the Board. The Board maintained that the carrier was wrong in refusing to allow the name of any organization to go on the ballot. "There is nothing in the Transportation Act to justify their course." The insistence of the carrier that no name should go on the ballot other than those of its employees was also held unjustifiable. The Board held that the employees could vote for representatives who were not employees of the carrier just as the carrier could select its representatives regardless of whether or not they were directors and stockholders. Furthermore, the Board denied the carrier the right to adopt regional division for representatives. "The Transportation Act contemplates that the class of employees directly interested on the entire system shall select their representatives, and even if it did not, the carrier would have no right to make such arrangement without the consent of the other contracting party."[1] The Board, however, declared that the election conducted by the labor organization was also illegal and void in that it was equally wrong for the union to suggest that the ballot should contain only the names of an organization to the exclusion of individuals.

The significance of the controversy was augmented upon the refusal of the carrier to comply with the decision of the Board to conduct a new election. The carrier denied that the Board had "power to prescribe an election or any other method by which the railroad may ascertain who are the authorized representatives of its employees."[2] The carrier stated that the contracts entered into between the representatives of both parties were to be in full force and effect. The duty of the Board had apparently been fulfilled, and the only obligation remaining was the publication of the decisions. This publicity the management of the road sought to avoid. A new chapter began when the matter became a controversy between the Pennsylvania Railroad and the Labor Board.

[1] *Railroad Labor Board Decisions* 1921, p. 220.

[2] *Railway Age Gazette*, 1921, vol. 71, No. 9, p. 399.

Taking the shop-craft dispute as a test case, the carrier obtained a temporary injunction against the Labor Board, restraining it from publishing the decision which was expected to charge the carrier with violation of the order of the Board. After several months of postponement, the United States District Court at Chicago sustained the position of the carrier and declared that the decisions of the Labor Board were only advisory, and that the Board had authority only in disputes jointly submitted by both parties.[1]

Thus stood the case until it was reversed by the Court of Appeals, whereupon the Pennsylvania Railroad appealed to the Supreme Court of the United States. The Supreme Court unanimously declared that the District Court was wrong in restraining the Labor Board from publishing its opinion. In delivering the opinion of the Court, Chief Justice Taft said that the Transportation Act "does vest the Labor Board with power to decide how such representatives ought to be chosen with a view to securing a satisfactory cooperation and leaves it to the two sides to accept or reject the decision."[2] Refuting the argument of the company that the Federation No, 90 was a labor union affiliated with the American Federation of Labor and that the phrase "organization of employees" used in the Act was not intended by Congress to include labor unions, Chief Justice Taft replied that there was "nothing in the Act to impose any limitation if the organization in other respects fulfils the description of the Act."[3]

The ruling of the Board was, therefore, greatly strengthened by the controversy. This liberal interpretation of

[1] *Op. cit.*, 1922, vol. 72, No. 17, p. 1022.

[2] 261 *U. S.*, 72 (1922).

[3] *Ibid.*, p. 82.

the Transportation Act augmented the power of the Board, but with the increase of power, the Board has exposed itself, in greater degree, to the attacks of both carrier and employees. Tendencies toward a modification of the system have already manifested themselves in many ways.

The late President Harding in his annual address to Congress, December 7, 1922, declared that the Labor Board was not constituted to best serve the public interest. His objection was that with six partisan members on a board of nine, it would inevitably follow that a partisan viewpoint would be maintained throughout all hearings and decisions handed down. Moreover, he believed that the work of the Board would be carried on better in Washington, and that the Transportation Act should be so amended as "to require the railroads and their employees to institute means and methods to negotiate between themselves their constantly arising differences, limiting appeals to the Government tribunal to disputes of such character as are likely to affect the public interest." In other words, President Harding recommended the following changes: (1) the establishment of a neutral board, the members of which should be non-partisan representatives; (2) that the work of the board should be carried on in Washington, and (3) that a law should be enacted to limit the number of appeals to the board.

The first suggestion of President Harding that the partisan membership should be abolished seems upon consideration quite unnecessary. While the Board would gain nothing by such reorganization, it would actually lose the valuable contributions of the partisan members. The arguments pro and con, which the neutral members might otherwise overlook, greatly help to clarify a situation. In this respect the participation of disputant parties in the board is beneficial. Moreover, the impossibility of adopting President Harding's proposal is very manifest. The carriers, on the one hand, will never consent to give up their right to participate in the settlement of matters of which they claim to have full and sole knowledge. The employees, on the other hand, will never accept any sort of arbitration which seems to them a tyrannic order coming from their superiors. For the Government to attempt such a restriction, furthermore, would involve great danger to the welfare of the public. What the railway workers demand is not dollars and cents alone. They strive for self-expression. If their representation in the Board is forfeited, they will take it as a direct oppression from the Government. Their participations in the Board have made possible the free expression of their views in their dealings with their employers. It would be extremely unwise for any political party to take away from the workers that right of expression.

The next proposal by President Harding, that the functions of the board would be better fulfilled if carried out in Washington, is not at all convincing. There seems to be no very good reason for the preference he expressed for Washington rather than Chicago, the center of railroad communication. The efficiency of the board would be greatly hampered if it sat in Washington by the distance from the center of railroad traffic. The danger of such a change is that the tribunal would more likely be carried into party politics, which would increase the difficulties of promoting better industrial relations.

President Harding was undoubtedly right in his assertion that the law should require the railroads and their employees to institute means to negotiate between themselves their constantly arising differences. The limitations of his recommendation that the law shall limit appeals to the Government tribunal to disputes of such character as are likely to affect the public welfare, however, should be carefully considered. For, in the first place, there is the difficulty of the interpretation of the law. Any dispute on the railroads may cause a strike and thus affect the public. In the second place, any discrimination as a result of the formulation of a law, will increase the misunderstanding between the disputants and the Government. If this be the case, the law will defeat the very purpose which it aims to accomplish. The only solution, therefore, is to increase the membership and working force of the Board so that some kind of division of labor among the members of the Board can be made.

President Coolidge, in his message to Congress, December 7, 1923, formulated no definite policy with regard to the Labor Board. He declared that "it has been a great help, but it is not altogether satisfactory." His conclusion in reference to the matter was that "if a substantial agreement can be reached among the groups interested, there should be no hesitation in enacting such agreement into law. If it is not reached, the Labor Board may very well be left for the present to protect the public welfare."

The Presidential election of 1924 marked an important episode in the life of the Railroad Labor Board. President Coolidge had no definite plan in mind as to the modification of the Transportation Act. He merely stated that the Labor Board had been an "interesting experiment" and that "it could probably be modified through mutual agreement to the benefit of all concerned."[1] Mr. Davis, the Democratic candidate for President, on the other hand, proposed two principles in the light of which the Esch-Cummins Law should be modified.[2] In the first place, any board for the adjustment of labor disputes "should consist of representatives of the employers on the one hand and representatives of the particular craft concerned in the controversy on the other . . ." In other words, the adjustment of labor disputes should be left to the parties themselves and there should be no representatives of the public on the board. The next principle was the creation of a new board for each individual dispute, for the reason that it would be better in every way that the boards "instead of being fixed in their personnel, should be filled by appointments made from time to time as the controversies arise."[3] Mr. Davis argued that nothing was more difficult than for a permanent board to retain the confidence of employers and employees. "Each decision it [a permanent board] is called upon to make exposes it to the charge of having unduly favored one side or the other, and is pointed to as a precedent when subsequent decisions are to be made." Senator La Follette, the Third Party candidate for President, pledged, in his campaign program, the abolition of the Labor Board. He had been an opponent of the labor provisions of the Transportation Act ever since its passage.

A bill[4] to provide for the abolition of the Railroad

[1] The statement was made in a speech delivered before a group of labor leaders who called at the White House on Labor Day, 1924.

[2] In a speech delivered before the Ohio Valley Trades and Labor Council, Labor Day, 1924.

[3] *Ibid.*

[4] *S.* 264b; H. 7358 (1924).

Labor Board was proposed in February, 1924, by Senator Howell in the Senate and by Representative Barkley in the House. The Howell-Barkley bill attempted to repeal Tittle III of the Transportation Act and offered a plan which consisted of machinery for conference, adjustment, mediation and arbitration. It provided that all disputes arising out of grievances or proposed changes in wages, rules or working conditions should be considered and "if possible, decided," in conference between the representatives of both parties. The representatives could be designated by any carrier or employees regardless of whether such representatives are individuals or organizations.

The next provision of this bill was the plan for the establishment of four adjustment boards. Adjustment Board No. 1 composed of seven representatives from the carrier and seven chosen from the engineers, firemen, hostlers, conductors, trainmen, switchmen, telegraphers, etc. Adjustment Board No. 2 also consisted of fourteen members equally representing the carrier on the one hand, and on the other the machinists, boilermakers, blacksmiths, sheet-metal workers, electrical workers, carmen and signalmen. Adjustment Board No. 3 required only six members, three from the carrier and three from the group of employees embracing the railway and steamship clerks, freight handlers, warehouse employees, stationary engineers, firemen, shop laborers, maintenance of way employees, etc. Adjustment Board No. 4 was to be composed also of six members representing equally the management and the employees. The labor representatives of the board were to be chosen from the following classes of employees: masters, mates, pilots, longshoremen, and marine engineers. All the members of these adjustment boards were to be nominated by the parties and selected by the President of the United States with the advice and consent of the Senate. Any of these boards could, for the purpose of efficient administration of its functions, at any time require the production of or have access to records and papers relating to matters which the board was empowered to consider.

Besides these adjustments boards, the bill proposed to establish a tribunal called the "Board of Mediation and Conciliation." This board was to consist of five members appointed by the President, with the advice and consent of the Senate. All the members of the board should have power to administer oaths and affirmations. In the case of any dispute upon the failure of the adjustment boards to effect a settlement and upon the request of either party, the matter should be referred to the Board of Mediation.

Should the efforts of the Board of Mediation be without avail in the settlement of a dispute, and in case both parties were agreed to arbitrate, the matter would then be adjusted by arbitration. The Board of Arbitration might consist of three or six members, with "power to issue subpoenas, require the attendance of witnesses and the production of such books . . . and documents" deemed necessary for the determination of the question. For the same purpose and to the same extent, the Board might invoke the aid of United States Courts to compel witnesses to attend and testify.

The difference between the labor provisions of the Transportation Act and this bill is that, according to the Transportation Act, the Labor Board can upon its own motion act on any dispute and make decisions leaving the parties the right to accept or to reject. But under this bill the board of arbitration could act only upon the agreement of both parties to arbitrate. It lays greater emphasis on conciliation and voluntary arbitration, and consequently labor organizations are in favor of its adoption. But in the eyes of the United States Chamber of Commerce, the bill has threatened " the fundamental principle of the paramount interest of the public." " It is based on the opposition of railroad employees and their organizations to the Railroad Labor Board and seeks to turn the clock backwards to the resumption of the former and weaker principles of mediation and conciliation."[1]

So far as the future is concerned, the continued existence of the Labor Board remains problematical. But so long as the Republican Party continues to control Congress, the expectation of any violent change in this field is visionary. It is fair to say that the existence of the Board depends on the continuance of the Republican administration as well as the Republican majority in Congress. Even taking these circumstances for granted, the destiny of the Board is determined by two other conditions, namely, the Board's own efficiency, on the one hand, and, on the other, the continuous tolerance of the parties concerned.

[1] Quoted in *Railway Age Gazette*, 1924, vol. 77, No. 21, p. 963.

CHAPTER IV

Compulsory Investigation in Canada

I. THE ANTECEDENTS OF THE INDUSTRIAL DISPUTES INVESTIGATION ACT

Canada, as early as 1900, had enacted an arbitration law, called the "Conciliation Act". While it proved a fair measure for settling disputes, it was found inadequate on many occasions. Its alleged success was based on the fact that during a period of seven years forty-six disputes were brought to a close through its agency.

The defect of the "Conciliation Act", however, was its failure to specify definitely whether the machinery for settling labor disputes was in reality mediation or arbitration. The Act placed emphasis on voluntary adjustment by allowing the parties to a dispute to decide whether the decision of a disinterested outsider, when chosen by and acceptable to both, should be regarded as final or merely as an intermediate step.

The year following the enactment of this measure a great railroad strike occurred. The test of the practicability of the law had come; and it failed to meet the test. In 1902, a bill was introduced by the Minister of Labor, providing for compulsory arbitration, but on account of bitter opposition from the labor organizations, the bill had to be withdrawn.

However, the Government felt that something should be done in order that serious disturbances might be avoided. As a result, the Railway Labor Disputes Act, called "an

Act to Aid in the Settlement of Railway Labor Disputes," was passed in 1903. By "railway" is meant all kinds of railways whether they are "operated by steam, electricity or other motive power." This Act created a Conciliation Committee and an Arbitration Board. The function of the Committee is to aid in conciliation or to mediate and make investigations. When a dispute is brought to the attention of the Minister of Labor, the Minister, upon the application of any of the parties to a dispute, or upon application of any municipality directly affected by the dispute, or upon his own motion, may form a committee of mediation, or of arbitration, or of investigation. Any such committee consists of three members, one recommended by the employers, one by the employees and the third, who shall be chairman, to be chosen by the two thus elected. Within five days, after notification from the Minister, each party to the dispute shall have nominated its representative, and in case of failure in such selection, the Minister of Labor shall himself appoint the representative. When a deadlock occurs in the selection of the chairman, the Minister also has the right to make the choice.

In case the committee fails to effect a settlement, the dispute may be referred to a Board of Arbitration. The establishment of the Arbitration Board may be effected in two ways: the mediators on the Committee may act as arbitrators, or a new board consisting of newly elected members may be formed. In the latter case, the manner of selection is to be similar to the method for selecting members of the Committee.

The results of the Railway Labor Disputes Act of 1903 were as encouraging as could be expected. In his report for 1907, the Minister of Labor asserted: "It is gratifying to be able to say that the statement made in previous reports of the department to the effect that since the passing of the

Railway Labor Disputes Act in July, 1903, there has not been a strike on any of the railroads of the Dominion of such a nature as to seriously effect transportation, still remains true, notwithstanding that another year has been added to the record."

In 1906, however, a prolonged strike of the coal miners at Lethbridge and Alberta occurred, beginning on March 9 and continuing until December 2 of the same year. Negotiations proved altogether fruitless. The "Conciliation Act" of 1900 failed in its final and severest test. The extension of the policy adopted toward railroad labor disputes to all public utilities came to be regarded as a necessity.

II. MACHINERY OF THE INDUSTRIAL DISPUTES INVESTIGATION ACT

This Act, passed in 1907, is "an act to aid the Prevention and Settlement of Strikes and Lockouts in Mines and Industries Connected with Public Utilities." It aims to extend the principle adopted in the Railway Labor Disputes Act of 1903.

A "Board of Conciliation and Investigation" is to be established in the same manner as prescribed in the law of 1903, though more restrictions and specifications have been made with respect to the constitution of the Board. No person who has pecuniary interest in a dispute shall be appointed to membership on a Board. The term of office of a Board begins with the date of appointment and terminates as soon as it has effected a settlement or reported its findings.

An application to the Minister of Labor for the forming of an Investigation Board, under the provisions of the principal act, requires statements setting forth certain facts relating to the disputes. The applicant is required to give the nature and cause of the dispute, and an approximate estimate of the number of persons affected or likely to be affected by the dispute, what efforts have been made by the parties to effect a settlement, etc.

When a deadlock occurs, both parties having failed to agree, the Board ascertains the facts concerning the case, and then makes a report to the Minister of Labor who has it printed for public distribution, and also published in the *Labour Gazette*. Any person who desires information regarding any case may apply for it to the Registrar of the Department of Labor.

No counsel or solicitor is permitted to appear before a Board without the consent of both parties, and even then a Board reserves its right to grant or not to grant such permission as it deems fit. A Board may also "dismiss any matter referred to it which it thinks frivolous or trivial."

Two important features of the law require special emphasis. These are the powers vested in a Board during its investigation, and the provision that strikes and lockouts "prior to and pending a reference to" a Board are illegal.

1. For the purpose of obtaining a full investigation, the Board is given all powers of summoning witnesses, compelling attendance and administering oaths. Furthermore, the Board may require the production of all books and papers to be examined by its members or experts whom it employs for that purpose. Documents shall not be made public, but the Board may obtain information from such documents and "in so far as it deems it expedient," may make this information public. All witnesses when summoned to appear before a Board concerning a railway labor dispute are entitled to free transportation. Proper certificates are issued by the Board to the persons who are entitled to such privilege. Failure to comply may subject the offending individual to a penalty of not exceeding one hundred dollars. Contempt of the Board in any proceeding also may subject the offend-

ing person to a fine of not exceeding one hundred dollars. A contempt of the Board includes wilful interruption of proceedings or wilful insult to the members of the Board or refusal to give evidence " without good cause."

2. The Act does not prohibit strikes and lockouts, but it does provide that a strike or lockout shall be unlawful during the process of investigation, or pending reference to a Board, or when a party is bound by an agreement. Furthermore, the relations between the parties to a dispute shall remain unchanged during the investigation.

Employers and employees shall give at least thirty days' notice of an intended change affecting conditions of employment with respect to wage or hours; and in every case where a dispute has been referred to a Board, until the dispute has been finally dealt with by the Board, neither of the parties nor the employees affected shall alter the conditions of employment with respect to wages or hours . . . [1]

Any violation of the provision described above subjects the offending person to a fine, in the case of a lockout, of not less than one hundred dollars nor more than one thousand dollars for each day that such a lockout exists, and in the case of a strike, of not less than ten dollars, nor more than fifty dollars for each day such strike continues.

The Investigation Act is designed especially, as indicated by its title, for mines and public service industries. But on joint application of both parties in any industry, the jurisdiction of the Act may be extended, and the parties then become bound by the provisions of the Act.

Amendments to this principal Act of 1907 have been enacted, but none of them has effected any radical change. In 1910, a clause was inserted altering slightly the form of

[1] Section 57.

the application for investigation. The applicant for the establishment of a Board must now state that attempts to adjust the dispute have failed, and that to the best of his knowledge a strike or lockout will be declared. He is furthermore required to state " that the necessary authority to declare such lockout or strike has been obtained." " Where a dispute directly effects employees in more than one province and such employees are members of a trade union having a general Committee authorized to carry on negotiations," a declaration must be issued by the chairman and secretary of such Committee to the effect that to the best of their knowledge a strike will be declared, that the dispute has been subject to negotiation, and that there is no hope of reaching a settlement. This amendment was intended to minimize the number of applications for investigations to the Minister of Labor.

In 1918, another amendment was added. It empowers the Minister of Labor to make inquiries when he thinks it is expedient and when a strike or lockout has occurred in any industry. The Minister of Labor may order an inquiry whether there has been application for it or not. It is further provided that even if no strike or lockout has occurred, he may " cause to be made any inquiries he thinks fit regarding industrial matters, and may cause such steps to be taken by his department and the officers thereof as seem calculated to secure industrial peace and to promote conditions favorable to settlement of disputes." [1]

Again, in 1920, a further amendment was made to the law. This change, also, has reference to the application for investigation. Additional emphasis is placed upon the dictum that the relations of the parties to a dispute should remain unaltered. The Minister of Labor " may on or without

[1] Canada: *Statutes*, 1918, chap. 27.

application order a Board or recommend inquiry." He does not have to find out that a strike or lockout has occurred in order to justify his action. Authorization to create a Board occurs whenever a strike or lockout "seems to the Minister to be imminent."

III. INTERPRETATION OF THE ACT

A better understanding of the important features of the Act may be obtained from an examination of the judgments handed down by the courts with respect to the operation of the Act. Sections 56, 57 and 60 of the Act are those of the greatest importance, and almost all the disputes which have arisen, have reference to the interpretation of these sections.

Charges of Inciting a Strike. The first appeal to the Court in regard to the Investigation Act was based on Section 60 prohibiting persons to incite employees to go on strike "prior to or pending a reference to a Board." "On September 6, 1907, James McGuire, president of the Cobalt Miners' Union was brought before the police magistrate at Cobalt, Ontario, on charge of inciting the employees of the Nipissing Mining Co. to go on strike contrary to Section 60 of the Act."[1] McGuire was found guilty and sentenced to a fine of $500 or in default thereof six months' imprisonment. The case was appealed to the Divisional Court at Toronto, which delivered the following judgment, declaring the conviction defective:

> The right of temporary interference with private liberty of action by the prohibition of lockouts and strikes during the period of actual investigation, as justified by the interest of the community being asserted by Parliament, there would be the less reason for non-interference before such investigation with a strike while, it might be disastrous, could only be shortlived,

[1] *Canadian Department of Labour Report*, 1908, p. 399.

inasmuch as it could be soon ended by the opposite party invoking the aid of the Act. In so far as the public interest is concerned in any restriction, it justifies even more the temporary prohibition *ab initio* than a mere interruption of the strike. The policy of the Act therefore does not assist, but equally with its terms, is opposed to the defendant's contention.

To come then to this particular conviction, as already mentioned, it makes no reference to the Act. It is impossible to gather from it that the defendant has been guilty of any offence. *Under some circumstances* [1] it is by this Act made unlawful to incite *some employees* of some employers to go on strike, but *not all employees nor under all circumstances.*

Outside of the Act, even where it may be unlawful in the sense of being actionable, it might not be a criminal offence or, even if a criminal offence, it might not be the subject of summary convictions.[2]

The Court declared, further, that there was nothing in the conviction of James McQuire to show that the incitement was prior to or during reference to a Board. A declaration of a strike on account of the dispute could not be found. The Court therefore declared the conviction defective.

Constitutionality of the Act Challenged. On November 11, 1912, the Superior Court of Montreal refused to grant a "Prohibition Order" to the Montreal Street Railway Company against the "Board of Conciliation and Investigation" established under the terms of the Act. The Company argued that the Industrial Investigation Act passed by the Federal Government was unconstitutional for the reason that the subject matter of the Act came exclusively under the jurisdiction of the Provincial Legislature. The Court, after due consideration, answered that the aim of the Investigation Act was to prevent strikes, and therefore could be

[1] My italics.

[2] *Labour Gazette*, 1907-1908, p. 1097.

applied to the whole country for the reason that a strike might cause nation-wide suffering. The social and economic condition of the country might be affected seriously by a strike which might cause disorder from one end of the country to the other. This "social and economic condition, as it affected multiform manifestations," extended beyond the limit of any one locality, and, therefore, it was of general character and not local or provincial.[1]

The Company appealed to the Court of Review for a final judgment.[2] This Court upheld the constitutionality of the Act but ordered the "Board of Conciliation and Investigation" to abstain from any further proceeding. The Act was held constitutional because its enactment came within the legislative powers of the Dominion Parliament. However, it reversed the decision of the Superior Court of Montreal, for the reason that "at the time of the application for the appointment of a Board of Conciliation and Investigation in this case, no dispute, within the purview or meaning of the Act, existed between the petitioner, the Montreal Street Railway Company, and any person or persons. . . ." Therefore, the Court maintained that "the Writ of Prohibition" could be issued.

The Thirty-days' Notice Clause. The thirty-days' notice clause has been used as a basic justification against dismissal. This clause declares that employers and employees shall give at least 30 days' notice of an intended change affecting conditions of employment with respect to wages and hours, etc. In July, 1915, a case was laid before the Police Magistrate of Vancouver, B. C., by the secretary of the local union No. 213 of the International Brotherhood of Electrical Workers of America, alleging that the British Columbia Electric Railway Co., Ltd., by the lockout of a number of

[1] *Op. cit.*, 1912-1913, pp. 629-630.

[2] *Ibid.*, 1913-1914, pp. 155-157.

electrical workers, had committed infringment of Section 57 of the Industrial Investigation Act. The opinion of the magistrate was that since the agreement between the parties after three years could be put to an end by a 90 days' notice in writing by one party to the other, the Company was, therefore, not bound by the agreement. The case was then brought to the County Court at Vancouver during October of the same year, but was adjourned several times until December. It then obtained a partial hearing. On account of technical objection made by the Counsel of the Company, the hearing was again delayed until January of the following year. Finally the presiding judge of the Court declared that he had no jurisdiction over this matter, and the case was finally dismissed.[1]

Another dispute concernig the observance of the 30 days' notice clause is the case instituted by the District Union No. 26 of the United Mine Workers of America against the Dominion Coal Company *et al.*, January, 1922. The miners applied to the District Court of Nova Scotia for an injunction restraining the Company from reducing the wages of their employees. The Court in making the decision alleged that the Act provides for a notice of thirty days' before any change affecting wages can be made. But the companies in this case gave a notice on December 18, 1921, and tried to make it effective on January 1, 1922. The notice was less than one half of the period provided for. "But the more important question is that presented by the fact that the notification of the proposed reduction has resulted in a dispute and that under the provision of Section 57 until that dispute has been finally dealt with by a Board of Conciliation no reduction as proposed can become effective."[2] The injunction was therefore granted in favor of the Union.

[1] *Op. cit.*, 1915-1916, p. 1056.

[2] *Ibid.*, 1922, p. 201.

The defendant companies appealed to the Supreme Court of Nova Scotia against the injunction. The Supreme Court sustained the appeal and declared that Section 57 of the Industrial Investigation Act applied when the change of conditions was brought about by "co-ercive action," and could not be enforced when the change of conditions occurred by the termination of a contract.

The history of the case was again cited, and the Supreme Court emphasized the fact that the change was a direct result of the termination of an agreement known as the "Montreal agreement" concerning the fixing of wages which was entered into between the parties in contention from November 8, 1920, until November 30, 1921. Both parties agreed that twenty days before the expiration of this Montreal agreement, they should meet in Halifax "for the purpose of arranging a new understanding." Consequently, in compliance with the agreement, the parties met on November 10, 1921, and mutually agreed upon the extension of the agreement for one additional month, or until the 31st of December. On December 16, the representatives of both parties met for the second time, and on this occasion the companies produced a schedule of wages which the Union refused to accept. On December 20, the companies notified their employees of the schedule making a wage reduction of 25 per cent. below the rates in the Montreal agreement. Basing their judgment on these facts, the Supreme Court delivered the following opinion: [1]

It was the expressed intention of the parties that existing conditions should terminate on the 31st of December. After that date unless a previous arrangement was made as provided in the several agreements it was obviously contemplated by both parties that the conditions of employment should be open and

[1] *Op. cit.*, 1922, p. 204.

unsettled. There is nothing I [Justice Mellish] think dealing with such a change in "conditions" as might arise by the *Co-ercive action* of either employer or employees and not with such as might arise by reason of the beginning or ending of the operation of such a contract as the Montreal agreement. The notices given by the defendants did not purport to change or alter any existing conditions. What they did propose was a schedule establishing new conditions to cover a period subsequent to the expiring of existing conditions on the date agreed on—a period as to which no conditions of employment had been settled either expressly or by implication.

IV. GENERAL RESULTS AND ESTIMATES OF THE SYSTEM

The Canadian Industrial Investigation Act has not succeeded in preventing strikes or lockouts, whether lawful or unlawful. There have been a number of violations of the restrictive provisions of the Act but only a few prosecutions for such offenses. Many strikes have occurred without any application being made to form an investigation board. Many strikes have taken place even in cases where applications had been presented. The appointment of a board requires time, and a strike, when voted for by men intolerant of existing conditions and determined to fight to the bitter end, must be declared at a certain time, and cannot be postponed if the desired aim is to be achieved. The law provides that when an application for investigation is made five days are given to the other party to nominate representatives and five additional days are allowed for the election of a chairman. The Board should be completed within fifteen days, but the Minister of Labor has discretionary power to extend this period. The result is that many of the boards require more than fifteen days for their formation. The Minister of Labor finds it necessary to use constantly his discretionary power. A number of boards have been established only after long hesitation for a period of two months.

The workers who have grievances to be corrected naturally resent the unnecessary delay.

According to the Canadian Department of Labor, the Act has had a successful record. From March, 1907, to March, 1924, there were 619 applications for investigation boards, and only in 37 cases were strikes not averted.[1]

With respect to the general estimates of the plan, no unanimous opinion can be obtained from either employers or employees. In spite of the opposition from both sides and in spite of the judgment of the Privy Council declaring the Act *ultra vires* of the Dominion Parliament, favorable opinions on the Act are not wanting.

The opinions of the employers generally are favorable to the Act. A law, in their estimation, no matter how imperfect it may be, is better than no law. Dr. V. S. Clark reported, after his investigation in 1908, that no employer was found who was not in favor of the law as better than no legislation so far as it applied to railways.[2] In his second report, in 1910,[3] Dr. Clark found again that "railway officers without an exception supported" the Act. The same held true of the mine managers of the East although some differences of opinion might be detected in the West where the operators were often "skeptical as to its value."

The indorsements of employers, like those of employees, were usually accompanied by some demand for amendment, and often the amendments suggested by the two sides were incompatible with each other. Upon the whole, during the last sixteen months, taking the whole Dominion into account, the Act has probably gained rather than lost in the esteem of employers, though in some cases unexpected weaknesses—from their point of view—have developed. However, these defects have been

[1] *Labour Gazette*, 1924, p. 646.

[2] *Ibid.*, September, 1908, p. 265.

[3] *Ibid.*, June, 1910, pp. 1388-1402.

more than counter-balanced by the gradual disappearance of that distrust with which a new law interfering in industrial matters is always regarded by those immediately affected. A year and a half ago, this distrust had a marked influence on the attitude of many large employers while in the summer of 1909, it was hardly observable.[1]

A good instance of the general approval of the Act occurred in the Association of Builders' Exchanges Convention, May, 1911. The Secretary-Treasurer of this convention, in his correspondence with the Minister of Labor, urged the extension of the scope of the Industrial Investigation Act. He recommended particularly that the Act should include the building trades, and in accordance with this recommendation, the Convention passed a resolution urging the Minister of Labor to take action to include the building trades within the competency of the Act. This was the second time such a resolution was passed, the first having been formulated by the same institution in its previous convention in 1910.

The opposition of employers to the Act probably can be summarized in the opinion expressed by a prominent mine operator in British Columbia. "It is my opinion that metal mine operators and smelter managers would have preferred that the Lemieux Act had not been passed, as they feel (as is apt to be the case in such acts) that the company will and can be legally and morally bound by its terms while there is not a great deal of likelihood that the unions will be bound or the Government will enforce fines and punishment upon the labouring men or the unions." [2]

But the opposition shrinks into insignificance when one considers the opinion of the Canadian Manufacturers' Association. The industrial relations committee of this associa-

[1] *Op. cit.*, June, 1910, p. 1393.

[2] *Ibid.*, September, 1908, p. 275.

tion reporting to an annual convention held at Montreal in June, 1924, said that the committee felt that "the Lemieux Act has proved of great benefit in the field which it was originally intended to cover. In support of this may be cited the fact that out of 580 disputes referred under the terms of the statute, there have been only 36 cases in which the threatened strike was not averted."

The opinion of labor organizations toward the Act are sharply divergent. Objections have been raised time and again by the Trade and Labor Congress of Canada. At the Twenty-fourth Annual Convention, September, 1908,[1] a resolution was submitted declaring that the working of the Industrial Disputes Investigation Act was "detrimental to Labour as a whole" and therefore that a demand for its repeal should be made. The resolution was referred to a committee which sent it back to the Congress without any recommendation. Finally a motion was adopted that the trades affected by the Act be requested to suggest amendments to the Act, and that in case the Government refused to make these necessary amendments, the Congress would pledge itself to abide by a referendum vote demanding to repeal the law.

Again at the Twenty-seventh Trade and Labor Congress, September, 1911, four resolutions proposing amendments to the Act and two resolutions demanding its repeal were introduced. After a lengthy debate, the Congress passed a measure calling for the repeal of the law. The declaration was as follows:

While this Congress still believes in the principle of investigation and conciliation, and while recognizing that benefits have accrued at times to various bodies of workmen under the operation of the Lemieux Act, yet in view of decisions and rulings

[1] *Op. cit.*, October, 1908, p. 403.

and delays of the Department of Labour in connection with the administration of the Act and in consequence of judicial decisions like that of Judge Townshend, in the Province of Nova Scotia, determining that feeding a starving man on strike is an offense under the Act: Be it resolved, that this Congress ask for the repeal of the Act.[1]

Similar discussion concerning the repeal of the law also occurred in the Twenty-eighth, Thirty-second, and other Congresses. But the opposition has been gradually growing weaker. Attention has been directed towards the amending of the law rather than towards its repeal. At every Congress, the Act has occupied an important part of the discussion. The recent tendency in the direction of demanding amendment may be illustrated by the proceedings of the Thirty-second Congress in 1922 in regard to the law, when no discussion took place for the repeal of the Act. The Committee on Resolution adopted the suggestion of Senator G. D. Robertson as follows:

In view of the fact that railway companies have violated Section 57 of the Industrial Investigation Act by putting into effect a reduction in wages to their employees after there was a dispute, and as there is no penalty attached to the section of the Act, be it resolved, that the executive council of the Congress use its best efforts to have the clause amended by imposing an adequate penalty on companies and corporations violating this section; . . . and be it further resolved, that the executive council be instructed to urge the Federal Government to amend the Act, making it compulsory upon the party seeking a change in wages or conditions to make application for a board in case an agreement is not reached.

The Act finds active supporters, also, among the labor unions. The Annual meeting of the Grand Council of the

[1] *Op. cit.*, December, 1911, p. 343.

Provincial Workmen's Association in 1912, highly approved of the Act calling it a "reasonable means of settling labour disputes, thereby securing as far as possible a continuity of that relationship which gives the best result to the employer and the employee, and leads to greater stability of trade and industry. . . ." The Council suggested a reform, however, declaring that efforts have been made to misapply the Act.

Again, the maintenance-of-way employees have upheld the Act as a good means for adjusting labor disputes. At their biennial convention in 1912, a resolution was passed containing the following statement:

> Resolved that this Grand Lodge assembled desired to be under stood as being emphatically in favour of the principle of the Industrial Disputes Investigation Act, which provides for investigation prior to any drastic action on the part of employers or employees as affected by the Act . . . [1]

The Canadian Federation of Labor also voices approval of the law. Among a dozen of resolutions adopted in the Fifth Annual Convention in October, 1913, declaration was made that the Act was "a good means of settling labour disputes." The Convention therefore resolved to re-affirm its confidence in the principle of the Act and to favor the extension of its scope.

V. THE ACT DECLARED UNCONSTITUTIONAL

The judgment of the Judicial Committee of the British Privy Council on the Toronto Electric Commission case, January 20, 1925, closes a chapter of the Canadian Industrial Investigation Act. The series of decisions which declare the statute invalid deserve a close examination.

A dispute occurred between the Toronto Electric Commission and its employees in June, 1923. The Commis-

[1] *Op. cit.*, December, 1912, p. 600.

sioners were a body corporate charged with the duty of the management and operation of the municipal electric light, heat and power work of the city of Toronto. The employees made application to the Minister of Labor for the appointment of a board of investigation. The application was legally granted, but the Toronto Electric Commission declined to recommend any person as its nominee to the board. Under the provision of Section 8 of the Act, the Minister of Labor made the appointment and announced the formation of a board of investigation. The commission protested against the board and challenged the authority of the Minister to appoint a member to the board. In spite of the protest, the board issued an appointment to proceed with the inquiry. Thereupon, the Commission petitioned for an interim injunction restraining the action of the board.

The injunction was granted. Justice Orde of the Supreme Court of Ontario, defending the injunction, declared that the Investigation Act and its amendments were in contradiction to the British North America Act which divides the power to legislate between the Dominion Parliament of Canada and the legislatures of the respective provinces. He said further that "certain co-ercive features" of the Investigation Act are interferences with civil rights of employers and employees. "The Board is empowered to summon witnesses, to compel the production of books, papers and other documents and to enter buildings and other premises for purposes of inspection, and to interrogate persons therein, and these powers are sanctioned by penalties for failure to attend or to give evidence or to permit inspection." The Act appeared to Justice Orde to have contained certain other features which were still more drastic, when he said that once the reference to a board of investigation was made, neither the employer nor the employee could put an end to a dispute by themselves, and that the employers must continue to pay the same wages. "It can hardly be suggested for a moment that these provisions are not a direct interference with the civil rights of the parties." He maintained, therefore, that the Act "purports to interfere in the most direct and positive manner with the civil rights of employers and employees and also with the municipal institutions" of the province.

Having possession of this favorable judgment, the Toronto Electric Commission applied for a permanent injunction restraining the board from making its investigation. The application, however, was refused this time. Justice Mowat handed down a judgment to the effect that the Act was within the powers of the Dominion Parliament. Justice Mowat argued that the question of industrial strife was "vastly different from the condition existing at the time of the passing of the British North America Act in 1867, and the silence of the Act regarding 'labour' and the absence of the specific allocation of that subject to the Dominion or the Provinces is thus accounted for." It appeared to him that labor legislation such as the Investigation Act was of national concern, and that it was important to distinguish between things of purely local and those of national concern. The Investigation Act met the needs of industrial strife which might affect the whole Dominion and therefore it should be brought within the jurisdiction of the Canadian Parliament.

The failure to obtain a permanent injunction against the board led the Toronto Electric Commission to appeal to the appellate division of the Supreme Court of Ontario. On April 22, 1924, Justice Ferguson delivered the opinion of the Divisional Court dissolving the injunction. This decision was concurred in by three other justices and only one justice dissented from the majority decision.

Justice Ferguson refuted the plaintiff's pleas that the Investigation Act was not within the powers conferred on the

Dominion Parliament by the British North America Act. He held that while the Act gave to the investigation board compulsory powers which encroached upon property and civil rights and involved in some cases, industries carried on by municipalities, according to the "true nature and effect of the enactment," in its pith and substance, the Act is a measure providing machinery for "investigation into industrial disputes between certain classes of employers and their employees, which disputes in some cases may and in other cases will develop into disputes affecting not merely the immediate parties thereto, but the national welfare, peace, order and safety, and the national trade and business."

The Justice maintained further that the legislation was of such nature as to fall within enumerated classes of Section 91 of the British North America Act. He argued that "employers" specified in subsection (c) of Section 2 of the Act were "dealers and venders in articles of trade and commerce, as well as producers thereof", and that the legislation might be read as being one preventing the interruption or suspension of industries of public necessity, by reason of their national importance. Not only could the legislation find its justification in the right of the Dominion Government to regulate trade and commerce, it could find support from criminal law as well. "The British North America Act does not confine the power of the Dominion to making criminal law, but the power extends to making law in relation to the criminal law." He went on to show that the Industrial Investigation Act was legislation designed for the prevention of crimes and for the protection of public safety, peace and order, and therefore could be supported by Section 91 of the British North America Act empowering the Dominion Parliament to enact laws "'in relation to' 'the regulation of trade and commerce', and to make laws 'in relation to' 'the Criminal law' 'in its widest sense'."

Justice Hodgins, dissenting from the majority opinion, declared that the case in question should be examined from three standpoints, namely, whether the statute could be supported "(1) under emergency, (2) as dealing with a matter of general Canadian interest and importance, and (3) whether under any enumerated head of jurisdiction it has been validly enacted." He held that the Statute failed to meet the first test in that it was based upon the normal condition of industrial relations and was not in any way designed to meet serious emergencies. In regard to the second consideration, he argued that the Act affected the Toronto Electric Commission which carried on its operations only within a province and that the Dominion Government should not interfere with what was in effect the rights specially reserved to the provinces to control their municipal institutions. Finally, he questioned the jurisdiction of the law on the ground that the relations of employers and employees resulting in production of commodities could not be included within the enumerated power of dealing with matters of trade and commerce. One of the enumerated powers of the Dominion Government, according to the justice, was to direct the movement and interchange of commodities and their purchase and sale, but not their production or manufacture or any of the conditions dealt with by this Act, which result in the production.

The adverse judgment of the Ontario Supreme Court was by no means final. The Commission continued its legal battle and carried the case to the Judicial Committee of the British Privy Council. On January 20, 1925, Viscount Haldane, delivering the decision of the Judicial Committee, said that the duty incumbent on the Judicial Committee was to interpret the British North America Act and to decide whether the statute in question was within the competence of the Dominion Parliament under the terms of Section 91 of that Act. "In this case the Judicial Committee have come to the conclusion that it was not." Viscount Haldane then proceeded to show that since the Act empowered the board to compel the production of books and documents, to render it unlawful for an employer to lockout or for a workman to strike prior to or during investigation and to impose obligation on the disputants to give thirty days' notice of any intended change affecting wages and hours, it was obvious that "these provisions dealt with civil rights, and it was not within the power of the Dominion Parliament to make this otherwise by imposing merely ancillary penalties."

The penalties for breach of the restrictions did not render the statute the less an interference with civil rights in its pith and substance. The Act is not one which aims at making striking generally a new crime. Moreover, the employer retains under the general common law a right to lockout, only slightly interfered with by the penalty. In this connection their Lordships are therefore of opinion that the validity of the Act cannot be sustained.

It is not necessary to investigate or determine whether a strike is per se a crime according to the law of England in 1792. . . . Let it be assumed that it was. It certainly was so only on the ground of conspiracy. But there is no conspiracy involved in lockout; and the statute under discussion deals with lockouts *pari ratione* as with strikes. It would be impossible, even if it were desirable, to separate the provisions as to strikes from those as to lockouts so as to make the one fall under the criminal law while the other remained outside it; and, therefore, in their Lordships' opinion this argument also fails.

Nor does the invocation of the specific power in Section 91 to regulate trade and commerce assist the Dominion contention. . . . It is, in their Lordships' opinion, now clear that excepting so far as the power can be invoked in aid of capacity conferred independently under other words in Section 91, the power to regulate trade and commerce cannot be relied on as enabling the Dominion Parliament to regulate civil rights in the provinces.

The Act was therefore declared *ultra vires* of the Dominion Parliament. Since then it has been amended to cover only disputes in relation to interprovincial transportation and other industries affected with a national interest.[1] While the scope of the Act has been greatly restricted, the principle of compulsory investigation thus still maintains its legal existence.

The merit of the system is that impartial investigation often brings about mutual understanding between the disputant parties. Arguments based on abstract principles seldom solve great difficulties. Labor disputes are matters of business relations which are capable of a compromise. By means of publication of findings, compulsory investigation helps to make the employers see the human side of their business and the employees the difficult problems which confront their employers.

The weakness of the system is not that the principle of public investigation is unsound, but that the reliance on public opinion for enforcement of awards is ineffective. True, when the public suffers losses and inconveniences, its interest may be aroused. But in a majority of cases the public is absolutely indifferent. The law requires the employees to defer their strikes at strategic times when they can use their power of collective bargaining most effectively. During the proceedings of investigation employers have the advantage of having ample time to make adequate preparation to meet any suspension. For the sake of guaranteeing justice to both sides, therefore, some provision requiring in definite terms the normal operation of business is highly desirable. The Canadian law provides that dur-

[1] Act of January 12, 1925.

ing an investigation conditions of employment should remain unaltered. But it does not go far enough to prevent employers from making preparation for industrial war. The strategy of time, while it means nothing to a lockout, means almost everything to a strike. It is to be hoped that the law will be amended in such a way as to give adequate protection to the legitimate interests of the employees.

CHAPTER V

Compulsory Arbitration in New Zealand

Turn now from the Western Hemisphere to a new continent—Australasia, where compulsory arbitration originated and where arbitral determination still grows and flourishes. The remaining portion of this monograph will deal with the chief features of compulsory arbitration laws, their provisions, their operation and their problems.

I. THE MACHINERY OF COMPULSORY ARBITRATION IN NEW ZEALAND

The enactment of the first compulsory arbitration law occurred in 1894. The history of the legislation goes back to the maritime strike of 1890 which had a widespread effect in New Zealand as well as in Australia. It was declared as a protest against a colonial shipping company for the dismissal of union officers. The colonial shipping companies, however, were in a strong position and determined to fight the strike to an end. The strike continued for three months. Public opinion voiced bitter condemnation of the strikers, seeing no reason why the seamen should strike merely because the Australian Maritime Council ordered a few of the strikers to quit. The strike finally failed, and the seamen were forced to accept terms favorable to the colonial shipping companies. This defeat on the part of the strikers paved the way for agitation for compulsory arbitration.

In the following year, 1891, a bill was drafted, providing for compulsory arbitration. It was passed three times by the House of Representatives, but the Upper Chamber each time rejected the bill on account of its compulsory character. Strong agitation on the part of the trade unions for the bill made it a campaign issue. The bill finally won a place on the statute book, and became effective August 31, 1894, but actual operation did not begin until the end of 1895.

This law of 1894, entitled "An Act to Encourage the Formation of Industrial Unions and Associations and to Facilitate the Settlement of Industrial Disputes by Conciliation and Arbitration," consists of five parts: Part I concerns the registration of industrial unions and associations; Part II has reference to industrial agreements; Part III concerns conciliation and arbitration; Part IV is on the subject of government railways; and Part V embodies diverse miscellaneous provisions. For an understanding of the essentials of this New Zealand system, a consideration of the first three parts will suffice.

1. Concerning registration, the Act provides that any number of employers or employees, not less than seven, may form an industrial union of employers or an industrial union of employees. An application for registration should contain a list of the members and officers of the society, two copies of the rules of the society and a resolution passed by the majority of the society indicating their willingness to be registered. No registration fee is rerequired. But any industrial society once registered becomes subject to the jurisdiction of the Act. Any industrial society might at any time apply for a cancellation of the registration, but such application would not be granted while a proceeding for conciliation or arbitration was in progress, and the cancellation would become effective only after a six weeks' public notice issued by the registrar.

Two or more industrial unions or societies may combine to form an industrial association. In the months of January and July of each year the industrial unions and industrial associations must report their membership to the registrar. In case of default, an industrial association is subject to a penalty of not exceeding two pounds for every week during which such default continues and each member of the council of the industrial association or union is also subject to a fine of not exceeding five shillings for every week during which he wilfully permits such default.

2. An industrial agreement may be formed between trade unions, industrial unions, industrial associations and employers. The term of an agreement should not exceed three years from the date of its formation. All agreements of this nature must be filed in the Supreme Court office, and the breach of their provisions makes the offending party liable to a fine of not exceeding five hundred pounds.

3. For purposes of conciliation and arbitration, the Governor of New Zealand is empowered by this Act to divide the colony into such industrial districts as he may see fit. In each of these industrial districts, the Governor should appoint a clerk of awards whose salary or other remuneration is left to the discretion of the Governor.

A board of conciliation is established in each industrial district to consist of an equal number of members from an industrial union of employees and from an industrial union of employers, the total number being left to the determination of the Governor. Three years are to constitute the term of office of these members and the chairman of the board is to be elected by the industrial unions. The board is vested with power to make all such investigations as are necessary to secure a fair settlement.

A court of arbitration is created, moreover, consisting of three members to be appointed by the Governor. One of the arbitrators must be recommended by the majority of the councils of industrial associations of employers, and one must be appointed upon the recommendation of the majority of the councils of industrial associations of employees, and the third is chosen from the judges of the Supreme Court. All arbitrators are to hold office for three years, and are to be eligible for reappointment.

Any award of the court is to remain binding on the parties to a dispute for a period not exceeding three years from the making thereof. Violation of any such award will subject the offending party or person to a fine not exceeding five hundred pounds in the case of an industrial union, and not exceeding ten pounds in the case of an individual on account of his membership in a union or an association.

When a dispute has been submitted to a board or to the court, no strike or lockout may take place until decision has been given. And even then, strikes and lockouts are unlawful if the unions are bound by agreements. This law has been repeatedly amended, but the principles of the act remain in spite of the amendments.

Minor amendments to the law previous to 1900 were enacted in 1895, 1896 and 1898. In 1895, it was provided that a minimum number of five employers could associate to form an industrial union of employers, and that two experts should be nominated to assist the court. The amending act of 1896 provided that no person, while sitting on one board, should be eligible for nomination to a seat on any other board. The amendment of 1898 made more explicit the power of the court to determine what constituted a breach of an award and what penalty might be attached thereto. The court was also given power to fix a minimum rate of wages.

The Consolidating Act of 1900 effected several changes: (1) The Act declared that the members of an industrial union of employers could claim a preference of service from unemployed members of an industrial union of workers, and the members of unions of workers could also claim to be employed in preference to non-members. (2) The Act, while retaining the original requirement of seven employees to form an industrial union of workers, reduced the minimum number of employers necessary to form an industrial union to two. (3) Until a dispute had been disposed of, neither the parties to the dispute nor parties affected by the dispute could do anything in the form of strike or lockout. Violation of the provision rendered the offender liable to a fine of fifty pounds. (4) The Court was empowered to extend its decisions to any part of the country, or the whole of New Zealand.

The amending act of 1901 again made two important changes with special reference to a definition of workers and industry, and to the legal procedure of appeal to the arbitration court. "Industry" was defined as meaning "any business, trade, manufacture, undertaking, calling or employment in which workers are employed," and a worker as "any person of any age of either sex employed by any employer to do any skilled or unskilled manual or clerical work for hire or reward." The original act did not make such specification of the terms, and on one occasion objection had come from the retail trades that the clerks and assistants in the retail trades were not under the jurisdiction of the act, because these trades were not "of an industrial character." This amending act aimed, therefore, at broadening the scope and power of the act in order to bring every employee and employer in the country, except those expressly exempted, under the jurisdiction of the law

Before 1901, every dispute was obliged to pass through a board of conciliation before it could be brought to the arbitration court, the purpose being to eliminate unnecessary burdens to the court and to employ conciliation as far as possible. In view of the small number of cases dealt with, however, the change was made that disputes could be brought directly to the board of arbitration.

Some regulative and minor changes were inserted into the law in 1903, 1905 and 1906, but not until 1908 did any change of importance take place.

The amendment of 1908 made various changes with regard to the jurisdiction of the act, the enforcement of awards and the method of procedure in the adjustment of disputes. A strike or lockout was declared unlawful when at its commencement the workers or the employers were bound by an award or industrial agreement affecting the industry in which the strike or the lockout occurred. While the penalties for strikes and lockouts remained the same as had been provided previously, emphasis was laid on special penalties to be incurred in the case of strikes and lockouts in industries which directly affect the production or transportation of necessaries of life. The specified industries were: (1) the manufacture or supply of coal-gas; (2) the production or supply of electricity for light and power; (3) the supply of water to the inhabitants of any borough or other places; (4) the supply of milk for domestic consumption; (5) the slaughtering or supply of meat for domestic consumption; (6) the sale or delivery of coal, whether for domestic or industrial purposes; (7) the working of any ferry, tramway or railway used for the public carriage of goods or passengers. Any person inciting or helping a strike or lockout in any of these industries became subject to a fine not exceeding twenty-five pounds. Any industrial union or industrial association or trade union committing the same offense was made subject to a fine of five hundred pounds.

The aot contained, moreover, a very rigid provision intended to prevent strikes and lockouts by the registered societies—the section, namely, which deals with the suspension of registration. Any industrial union or industrial association, when it has been convicted of having committed an unlawful strike shall be suspended from registration for a period not exceeding two years. During the period of suspension, such organization shall be incapable of instituting or being a party to any conciliation or arbitration proceeding. Neither shall it be allowed the privilege of cancelling its registration nor shall a new industrial union or industrial association of workers be registered in the same industrial district to include the same industry. On the other hand, interpretation of the law makes strikes and lockouts lawful for non-registered unions, and strikes also may take place after the cancellation of registration.

The act provides in addition for the enforcement of awards and industrial agreements, as may be found in part II, Section 13, "Every industrial union, industrial association or employer who commits a breach of an award or industrial agreement shall be liable to a penalty not exceeding one hundred pounds in respect of every such breach," and every worker to a penalty not exceeding five pounds. The dispute may be brought before a magistrate, and then to the arbitration court.

The most significant changes made by this act have reference to conciliation, namely, the substitution of a "conciliation council" for the old "board of conciliation" which had previously operated. All provisions relating to the board were repealed, and new methods for conciliation, a method which had been generally disregarded since the amending act of 1901, were introduced. The principal change made by the new provisions was that no industrial dispute should be referred to the arbitration court until it had been first passed upon by a council of conciliation.

A council of conciliation, as provided in the law of 1908, is made up of a commissioner of conciliation and a number of assessors. The Governor of New Zealand has full power to appoint conciliation commissioners. Each commisssioner is assigned to a particular industrial district determined by the Governor, and exercises his powers within his district. His term of office is three years and he receives remuneration for his services as appropriated by Parliament. Not more than four such commissioners may be appointed at any one time. In case disputes arise in a district where no commissioner is immediately available, the Governor may either order any of the commissioners already appointed to perform the duty or appoint some person to act as a commissioner for the purpose of dealing with such disputes.

The assessors are appointed only after a dispute arises, and their selection is made from persons recommended by each disputant party. The number of assessors is determined upon the recommendation of the applicants for conciliation but such recommendation must have the approval of the commissioner. An assessor so recommended "may be one of the parties to the dispute or may be a member of an industrial union or industrial association which is a party to the dispute." Any of the assessors so recommended may be disqualified by the commissioner, and under such circumstances, the applicants shall recommend other qualified persons to take their place. In case of the death or resignation of an assessor, a new assessor is to be appointed upon the recommendation of the applicant or the respondents as the case may be. If a deadlock occurs with regard to such recommendation the commissioner may appoint a qualified person so recommended.

The powers and duties of the council are clearly defined It has the power to make inquiries either public or private as it may see fit. But at any such inquiry before the council no person is bound "to give evidence with regard to trade secrets, profits, losses, receipts, or outgoings in his business, or with respect to his financial position, or to produce the books kept by him in connection with his business." But if any person desires to give evidence by producing his books, he may do so to the commissioner alone and not the assessors, and the commissioner shall not disclose to the assessors any such secrets or particulars, but he is at liberty to express his opinion whether or not a claim or allegation made by any of the parties is substantiated by the evidence. In case any one of the parties to a dispute fails to attend at any inquiry, the council, if representatives have been appointed for the absentee party, may proceed with the inquiry. "If no settlement of the dispute is arrived at by the parties in the course of the inquiry, the council shall endeavour to induce the parties to agree to some temporary and provisional arrangement until the dispute can be determined by the Court of Arbitration." The council may offer a recommendation for the settlement of the dispute, but "no such recommendation shall be made unless it is unanimously agreed to by all the assessors, and the commissioner shall have no vote in respect of the making or nature of any such recommendation."

II. GENERAL RESULT OF THE EXPERIMENT

While the New Zealand experiment can by no means be regarded as a complete success, in the light of its results, it has certainly accomplished some degree of success. The experiment has passed through three distinct periods:

The first period began with the enactment of the law in 1894 and continued until the Consolidation Act of 1901. During these six years the act received the whole-hearted support of the workers involved, and in fact, the law of 1894 was largely a result of political action on the part of the industrial workers. The boards of conciliation in this period effected continued advances in wages, and in many cases reductions of hours, and improvements in working conditions. The laborers began to appreciate the profitableness of appealing to the Arbitration Court for the adjustment of disputes rather than engaging in expensive and destructive battles. New Zealand came to be called "a country without strikes," and certainly, for a number of years, it deserved the good name. From 1894 to 1905, New Zealand enjoyed an unparalleled period of industrial peace, during which there were actually no strikes. The workers realized that no better results could be obtained by means of strikes than by accepting the awards of the conciliation boards and the court of arbitration.

The employers, on the other hand, strongly opposed the law and its operation. They felt that the law had infringed upon their individual rights, and asserted that it was designed to penalize one class for the advantage of another. Their successful efforts in defeating similar bills before 1894 indicate the strength and persistence of their objections. When the law of 1894 went into operation, employers in many cases refused to send representatives to the boards of conciliation, and the government exercising its prerogatives, appointed representatives for them; but such compulsion at the outset destroyed the principle of conciliation. The employers' failure to cooperate, therefore, may be held responsible for the eventual failure of the boards of conciliation.

The opposition of the employers to the law at this period was best exemplified by the criticism of several New Zealand employers' organizations of the Victorian commission which investigated the operation of the New Zealand law and reported that there was in New Zealand a unanimous opinion in favor of the Act. Statistical evidence was compiled to refute the commission's report. Employers in different parts of New Zealand were requested to answer a set of questions. When the question was asked whether in their opinion the Act had been the cause of creating disputes, only three employers replied in the negative.[1] When the question was asked whether the Act had helped to increase the general prosperity of the country, only one employer answered affirmatively. Again questions relating to operation of business were asked: (1) whether the Act had increased the expenses of business and therefore decreased the amount of profit; (2) whether the Act had discouraged or prevented the investment of capital in industries. The replies to both of these questions were in the affirmative with only one negative answer in each case.

Officers of several employers' organizations expressed their objections to the Act. The president of the Canterbury Employers' Association, refuting the statement of the Victorian Commission, said that if the principle of the Act was the substitution of arbitration for strikes, the employers were in favor of it, but that if it entitled workingmen to interfere with the management of their business, they were unquestionably against it. "If sweeping the Act out of existence would restore the old order of things, we would strain every nerve to do it. . . ." The secretary of the Wellington Employers' Association, in criticising the Act, said that the actual effect of the Act had been a standardization of all matters concerning employment in minutest detail; "in fact, to a very large extent, the conduct of a man's business is taken out of his hands and placed under the control of a court." The secretary of the New Zealand Iron Masters' Association expressed a similar opinion when he asserted that the conciliation board had failed to adjust disputes and that it was ridiculous to expect harmonious relations when by the very nature

[1] Victorian Employers' Federation, *Compulsory Conciliation and Arbitration, Case Against Them* [employers], 1907, p. 7.

of the Act, employer and employees were put into two hostile camps. He was of the opinion that "the majority of the business people" held that the Act had failed to accomplish what was expected. These opinions were fairly representtive. The employers, according to these views, preferred the strike to mediation and arbitration, which meant, to a certain extent, interference with their businesses.

The second period extended from the Consolidation Act of 1901 to the amending act of 1908, and is characterized by growing dissatisfaction on the part of the workers. The procedure of conciliation had been changed. Cases were piling up in the arbitration court, and the resulting congestion caused unnecessary delay in reaching any settlement, contributing to the general discontent. Moreover, the awards of the arbitration court proved in many cases unsatisfactory to the workers.

At the annual Trades Councils' Conference, in April, 1906, opinion was expressed by a Wellington delegate that the conference should resolve that it had no confidence in the arbitration court in view of the fact that in many cases the court had "given its judgment without any consideration of the evidence, and without any reference to the evidence of both parties."[1] A Dunedin delegate assented to this opinion and added "they were getting too much law and too little justice." These and other statements express well the current opinion at the time.

As a result of the unrest, the first strike since 1894 occurred in November, 1906,[2] and although not the result of direct dissatisfaction with an award of the Arbitration Court, it was indirectly influenced by the general discontent

[1] Quoted in Broadhead: *State Regulation of Labour and Labour Disputes.*

[2] This was a strike against the Auckland Tramway Co. The Company discharged two employees. The motormen struck in protest.

with the court. The men were in a fighting mood and sometimes declared a strike without first appealing to the court. The following year, according to the figures of the New Zealand Official Year Book, was marked by six more strikes.

The workers believed that conciliation should play the more important part in the adjustment of their differences, and that only as a last resort should arbitration be invoked, for from 1902-1908 there were only 22 cases adjusted by conciliation while 372 cases or 94.4 per cent went to arbitration; while during the first period of the operation of the Act 51 cases had been adjusted by conciliation and 100 cases were settled by arbitration. An official manifesto of the Wellington Trades and Labor Council, July 2, 1908, emphasized the need of boards of conciliation and also expressed the workers' opposition to the court:

We want the act as originally conceived by the framer. . . . The failure of the present act is due to the fact that employers have designedly ignored the Boards [of conciliation] and relied on the Court [of arbitration]. The Constitution of the Court, with its legal encumbrances and formula and the unconscious bias of its president, makes the odds two to one against the workers every time. The Court has of late, in addition to its failure to improve the industrial condition of workers, attempted to usurp the power of depriving the worker of constitutional rights already granted. We for the time being advise the workers to adhere to the principle. As an improved method of settling industrial disputes conciliation has always been advocated by the workers, and we again urge the importance of it. Only as a last resort should the Court, in our opinion, be resorted to.[1]

The third period of the experiment commenced with the amendment of 1908, which repealed the Act of 1901 and

[1] Quoted in Icholefield, G. H., *New Zealand in Evolution*, p. 240.

reestablished the formal procedure of the boards of conciliation. A change in the law occurred in 1915, when the New Zealand Parliament passed the Cost of Living Act. This Act created the Board of Trade which was to investigate conditions in industry and commerce and the cost of living in the colony. The section of the law in regard to the inquiry into the cost of living affected the decisions of the Court of Arbitration, in that thereafter the element of the cost of living in the adjustment of wages definitely came into great prominence.

The "Alliance of Labour" has in recent years been strongly against the Act. The first important movement for the abolition of the Law was launched in December, 1923, after the Court had been sitting at Wellington on cases involving demands for reductions of wages. At this sitting the Alliance asked for an opportunity to be heard in support of an application for a general order to increase wages, the reason for the petition being that the Court had been misinformed on some matter concerning some statistical calculation of rent. The Court granted the request, with the condition that the Alliance could arrange a date with the Employers' Federation to meet at Auckland. The latter organization, however, refused to reopen the discussion. The Alliance then requested the Court to hear its representatives alone, but this the Court declined to do. This refusal, in the eyes of the workers, was a glaring injustice. Their denunciation of the system of arbitration grew more and more vigorous.

The employers, on the other hand, have come to uphold the law. They by no means consider the system as perfect, but they have taken the position of defending the Act and at the same time suggesting amendments which would work to their best interest Thus, one officer of the Employers' Federation, praising the Act as having benefited the people of New Zealand, went so far as to say that it was because of the Act that New Zealand had comparatively less industrial strife, while England and America were suffering an enormous amount of unemployment and considerable strife. He declared that the system of compulsory arbitration regulated the industrial conditions of the country. "In New Zealand the Arbitration Court acted as a brake on wage movements. It steadied wages on both the up-grade and the down-grade with the result that wages did not reach an extraordinarily high peak or later fall to an abnormally low level."

The general policies of the Court can be briefly summarized in a few words. The question of hours, wages, union preference, working conditions, apprenticeship and treatment for under-rate workers are some of the chief problems.

1. The eight-hour day has long been accepted as a fair measure of the working day. In several industries, the forty-four-hour week has also been adopted for some time. There are exceptions, however, as when the Court has refused to fix definite working hours and left the matter to voluntary agreement between the employers and the employed. The forty-four-hour week has not yet been adopted in the street railway industry.

2. With respect to the matter of wages, a minimum wage has been determined for every industry, and no employer can pay less than the legal wage without becoming liable to suit for breach of award, and appropriate penalties on conviction. The Court has complete power to fix wages and enforce its awards within the jurisdiction of the Arbitration Act. The cost of living differs slightly in different parts of New Zealand, and in the adjustment of a scale of wages, the Court tends to make uniform increases to workers in similar industries irrespective of the differences of living conditions in various parts of the country. The Court has

established a policy of granting only conservative advances in wages and conservative reductions in wages, in spite of the many petitions from the employees for increases and from employers for wage reductions.

3. Union preference has generally been prescribed by the Court with the condition that the union is required to permit any worker of "good character and sober habits" to become a member upon payment of the entrance fee and other lawful contributions.[1] The Seamen's Union fought for union preference soon after the Act was in operation. But even as late as 1906 preference was not yet granted. In the Dunedin Seamen Case [2] one of the assessors dissented from the decision of the Court, saying that "a good case has been made for preference to unionists; over 95 per cent of the men employed being members of the union. . . ." The Court held, however, that the granting of preference to seamen would interfere with the discipline on board ship. But in recent years, union preference has generally been granted to seamen, though there are conditions which the union must observe in order to be entitled to this privilege. Union members could have preference only so long as their union did not "order, encourage, aid or abet any strike, job-control, or obstruction of any kind or disregard any decision of the Dispute Committee on any matter referred to it, or do anything to defeat the provision of this award." [3]

4. General working conditions have been regulated in great detail. Emphasis has been placed upon the presence of sanitary conditions in workshops and factories. In the mining industry, for instance, water must be removed as far as possible from the place of work, and when this cannot be

[1] New Zealand Department of Labour, *Annual Reports of Awards*, 1897, p. 296.

[2] *Ibid.*, 1906, p. 50.

[3] *Ibid.*, 1922, p. 1002.

done, the workman is entitled to extra pay. Government regulations require that a certain standard of ventilation be maintained.

5. There are a variety of rules for apprenticeship in different trades, but the obligations of the employer to his apprentices remain in almost all cases the same. The employer cannot dismiss them during the course of their apprenticeship because of slackness of work, although he may transfer them from one class of work to another because of such slackness. Whenever an apprentice is discharged, the employer should notify the Inspector of Factories, giving the cause of the dismissal.

6. Any worker who for any reason becomes incapable of earning a minimum wage, upon application to the union and after due notice to the Inspector of Factories, may receive a lower wage, after a hearing of evidence from the union and the employer concerning the case, the Inspector of Factories or any person appointed by the Arbitration Court for the purpose shall fix a wage for the under-rate worker, but shall take into account the worker's capability, his past earnings and other circumstances. Except in cases of old age or permanent disability, when wages may be determined for as long a period as the Inspector of Factories may see fit, the wages for ordinary under-rate workers shall be fixed for a period of not exceeding six months, after which time readjustment will be made.

III. MERITS AND DEMERITS OF THE SYSTEM

Whether compulsory arbitration will continue to flourish in the fertile soil of New Zealand or be transplanted from its original abode to other lands or be totally abolished, the result will influence markedly the present industrial order. It is of great importance that students of economics should give this system careful consideration and find out its advantages and disadvantages.

The Arbitration Court of New Zealand has accomplished many reforms. It has succeeded in making through-going investigations of labor conditions and by means of its findings has made known the grievances of both employers and employees. Moreover, upon the basis of its official findings, the Court has gradually achieved progressive measures, including the granting of union preference, the shortening of hours, together with the increasing of wages and the improvement of working conditions. These progressive advances speak for themselves. They indicate that the Court has been a powerful friend to the weaker and poorer labor groups, which in the absence of compulsory arbitration could hardly have achieved their present state, especially with regard to the living wage, forty-four-hour week and union preference. Even the strong unions too are indebted to the Arbitration Court. True, in many cases the Court fails to adjust grievances, but, on the whole, the unions have won substantial gains because of the existence of compulsory arbitration.

Even the employers, when not giving rein to their prejudices and obstinacies, cannot condemn the system, as it has operated in New Zealand, for having impaired or driven away trades and industries from the country. The industrial and business world of New Zealand has its ups and downs just as the tides of prosperity and depression have their ebbs and flows in other parts of the world. New Zealand has so far never suffered any industrial crisis more severe than those elsewhere. It does not require a radical mind to appreciate the value of the system. The President of the Employers' Federation in the nineteenth annual convention in 1921 declared, "On the whole, with all its defects, the New Zealand system of arbitration has worked better than any system devised elsewhere for the same end." [1]

[1] *Industrial Bulletin*, December 6, 1921, p. 11.

Another officer of the Federation, addressing the annual convention of the organization in 1924, declared that the New Zealand system of arbitration had been "the simplest, sanest and safest method of regulating industrial conditions in any part of the world." [1]

On the other hand, the New Zealand system of compulsory arbitration has its defects as well as its merits. The Act has failed in the prevention of strikes and lockouts. The Act itself permits the occurrence of strikes by unregistered unions. Any union can refuse registration and be free from the interference of the arbitration Court. Even though unions do register and promise to abide by the decision of the Court, enforcement of the penal provisions has been impracticable in connection with the great strikes declared by large unions, because the number of people involved makes it an impossible task for the Court to collect fines or order penalties of imprisonment. True, in small strikes, the penalties of the Act may be applied, but that is not justice, nor is it a principle of good government. The failure in the enforcement of the Law is not only unfair to employers, but also most unfair to workers as well. When of two unions both pledged to abide by the judgment of the Court and both guilty of violating the law, one is penalized for the breach of promise and the other escapes punishment simply because of its size, the injustice committed is too obvious to require discussion.

Another defect of the system arises from the heavy task imposed upon the Court. The judges are responsible for all the details affecting the working population as well as the employing classes in the whole country. In fact, each of the two partisan members of the Court naturally speaks for the interests of his group, and the decision is actually rendered by one man. By what means and capacity can any

[1] *Op. cit.*, August 11, 1924, p. 66.

one man rightly and faithfully discharge a duty which is so complicated and forever changing in character and complexity? Although New Zealand has now a population of only 1,316,159, (Census of December 31, 1924) and the Court has, therefore, been able to achieve some degree of success, yet it would be difficult to guarantee its efficiency as the population increases. It may be argued that efficiency can be maintained by an increase of the number of judges as the population increases. Yet the rapid growth of industries may offset the proportional increase of the Court's efficiency. The large capital involved and the complexity of the industrial operation may render the application of compulsory arbitration impracticable. It would be a dangerous step, therefore, for any state at an advanced industrial stage to enter upon the New Zealand road of compulsory arbitration. The peculiarly favorable circumstances, a small population, a sustained demand for labor, and an isolated situation, which prevail in New Zealand, may justify the existence of compulsory arbitration in that country, but the absence of these circumstances in other countries points decisively against the adoption of this plan

Professor Alfred Marshall has clearly sounded a brief warning against the adoption of such a measure in England when he says: " Australasia has indeed a great reserve of borrowing power in her vast landed property: and should the proposed short cuts issue in some industrial decadence, the fall may be slight and temporary. But it is already being urged that England should move on similar lines: and a fall for her would be more serious." [1]

[1] Marshall, *Principles of Economics*, eighth edition, p. 45.

CHAPTER VI

Compulsory Arbitration in Australia

I. COMPULSORY ARBITRATION IN SOUTH AUSTRALIA AND OTHER STATES

Contrary to prevailing opinion, compulsory arbitration originated not in New Zealand, nor in New South Wales, but in the less familiar state of South Australia. True, the system of compulsory arbitration won its legal recognition for the first time in New Zealand; then it found its way back to Australia, first in New South Wales in 1901, then in Western Australia in 1902, then in the Commonwealth of Australia in 1904 and finally, in 1912, back to South Australia. However, it owes its birth to South Australia though it bears a debt equally great to New Zealand for its first adoption.

The father of the system was Charles Cameron Kingston who for some years had been Premier of South Australia and afterwards a member of the Australian Commonwealth Parliament. He introduced a bill providing for compulsory arbitration in the South Australian Parliament on December 12, 1890. The title of the Act was identically the same as that which was later enacted by New Zealand, with the exception of the phrase "by Conciliation and Arbitration" in the latter case. It read "An Act to Encourage the Formation of Industrial Unions and Associations and to Facilitate the Settlement of Industrial Disputes." The provisions of the Act were also identical, with few exceptions, to the New Zealand Law of 1894. It called for registration of industrial unions and associations. It provided for conciliation as well as for compulsory arbitration and enforcement by penalty of fine or imprisonment in case of default. The only measure which W. Pember Reeves, the author of the New Zealand system, rejected was the section providing for the erection of a "Conciliation Hall." The Kingston Bill required the Government of South Australia to grant a block of land in the city of Adelaide for the purpose of erecting a hall to be called "Conciliation Hall." The failure of this bill was attributed partly to the requirement of this section and largely to the unpreparedness of public opinion to support the bill.

Nevertheless, the system came back to South Australia in 1912. The "Industrial Court Act" of 1912 repealed the Conciliation Act of 1894 and proposed "to make better provisions for dealing with Industrial Matters and Disputes. . . ." The Act created a tribunal, called the Industrial Court, which consists of three members with a judge of the Supreme Court as its president. The Court possesses power to intervene in all industrial disputes and make decisions for their settlement.

In rendering any decision, the Act requires the Court to "absolutely secure" a living wage which should be "a sum sufficient for the normal and reasonable needs of the average employee's living in the locality where the work under consideration is done or is to be done." It outlaws all strikes and lockouts. Any person or association who or which attempts anything in the nature of a strike or lockout "shall be liable to a penalty not exceeding five hundred pounds, or, in the case of a person, to imprisonment, with or without hard labor, for a term not exceeding three months." The penal feature of the Law applies, therefore, with absolute equality to both employer and employee.

Two amendments were incorporated into the Act in 1915 and 1916. These two amendments together with the principal Act of 1912 form an act called the "Industrial Arbitration Acts 1912 to 1916." The amendment of 1915 makes further provision with respect to registration of industrial unions, the procedure of registration and the conditions under which cancellation of registration shall occur. The amendment of 1916 calls for the appointment of a "deputy president" to assist the president of the Industrial Court. All these acts were finally consolidated in 1920.

Under the Industrial Code of 1920, which consolidated all laws relating to industrial matters, three closely related organizations simultaneously function. They are, namely, the "Industrial Boards," the "Industrial Court," and the "Board of Industry." The Industrial Boards superseded the wage boards created by previous statutes. The function and constitution of the Industrial Court remains exactly the same as in the former Acts of 1912 to 1916. The Board of Industry, however, is a new creature brought into being by the Industrial Code. Its function is the coordination of the operation and the administration of the industrial boards and the Industrial Court.

An industrial board may be created in any industry upon the recommendation of the Board of Industry. The industrial board so created may consist of four, six or eight members besides the chairman, as the Board of Industry may recommend. The membership of the board is composed of an equal number of representatives from the management and the employed. Within seven days after their appointment these representatives choose a chairman, and in case of a deadlock, the "President of the Board of Industry" appoints the chairman. After its formation the board is empowered to fix wages, hours of employment and working conditions. In the matter of fixing wages, it may take into consideration the following factors:

(a) The nature, kind, and class of work;
(b) The mode and manner in which the work is to be done;
(c) The age and sex of the employees and in addition, as regards apprentices and improvers, their experience in industry;
(d) The place and locality where the work is to be done;
(e) The hour of the day or night when the work is to be done;
(f) Whether more than six consecutive days' work is to be done;
(g) Whether the work is casual as defined by the Board [Industrial Board];
(h) Any recognized usage or custom in the manner of carrying out the work;
(i) Any matter or thing prescribed.[1]

The Industrial Court is a court of appeal. Any industrial dispute, the adjustment of which fails in an industrial board, may be appealed to the Industrial Court for settlement, provided that the determination of the board has not yet been published in the *Government Gazette.* The Court consists of a president, or a deputy-president, who shall hold office for seven years and not be removed from office except in the same manner and upon such grounds as a judge of the Supreme Court is by law liable for removal. The president of the Court may for purpose of obtaining assistance, appoint two assessors to sit with him at the hearing. These assessors within three years previous to their appointment must have been bona-fide employees or employers in the industry from which the dispute arose. The Court possesses the power to determine the rate of wages, the number of hours and other industrial questions, but the question of granting union preference is expressly declared to be outside of its jurisdiction. The decisions of the Court on all matters are final and "shall not be removable to any other court by *certiorari* or otherwise."

[1] South Australia, *Statutes*, 1920, no. 1453, p. 72.

The Board of Industry is composed of a president or a deputy-president and four commissioners, two representing employers and two representing employees. The functions of the Board include classifying industries, making recommendations to the Minister of Industry in regard to the appointment of industrial boards, declaring a living wage and performing other duties from time to time assigned to it by Parliament.

This system of adjustment manifests clearly its compulsory character. The substitution of the industrial boards for the wage boards means the abandonment of the process of conciliation and the adoption of compulsory conferences. The Industrial Court controls every industrial matter which may be subject to controversy; in fact every industrial matter that exists.

Two other states of the Australian Commonwealth, namely, Western Australia and Tasmania, have adopted systems resembling so closely those of other more important states that a detailed discussion of the two systems in these pages is unnecessary. It should be noted in passing, however, that compulsory arbitration was first introduced into Western Australia in 1900, and the act was amended in 1902 and again in 1912. The Industrial Arbitration Act of 1912 provides for legislation for industrial unions and associations and requires the settlement of industrial disputes before the Court of Arbitration. This arbitration Court consists of three members—a judge from the State Supreme Court and two other members one representing employers and one representing employees, to be nominated by the respective groups and appointed by the Governor. Some minor changes were inserted into the Act in 1920, but none of these changes affect any important provision of the principal Act.

It should be observed also that Tasmania inaugurated the

wage-board system in 1910, and that it has been following the example of Victoria which originated the wage-board system.

II. THE WAGE BOARD SYSTEM OF VICTORIA

The development of the wage board system in Victoria finds its origin in a series of Factories and Shops acts enacted in 1890, 1896, 1898 and 1900, which had as their object the elimination of the sweating system. Public agitation against the evils of sweating led to the appointment of a parliamentary board in 1893 to make inquiries and report on the working of the Factories and Shops Act of 1890 with regard to sweating practices.

In 1896 provision for special boards, or wage boards, as they are generally called, first made its appearance. This act of 1896 was to remain in force for four years, and special boards were created for four of the worst sweated trades: clothing, boots and shoes, furniture, and bread baking. After the expiration of that term, it was renewed for a further probationary period of two years. In 1900, a Royal Commission was appointed to inquire into the workings of the special boards and to investigate the operation of similar laws in other Australian states, as a result of which the Commission recommended the abolition of the wage-board system and the adoption of compulsory arbitration on the New Zealand model.

The employers were bitterly opposed to the introduction of compulsory arbitration. After the Royal Commission had made its report concerning the operation of the New Zealand system, the Employers' Federation of Victoria officially declared that the New Zealand legislation was "mad". "Can producers, employers, and trades be harassed in this way without checking enterprise, curtailing employment, and giving this State a heavy handicap in the

Commonwealth?"[1] In this declaration the Federation also appealed to individual employers for support and said that if the people of the Australian Commonwealth, and particularly Victoria, were not prepared to hand over the control to their business interests, a vigorous opposition must be offered. "*The danger is pressing. Do not be led away with the specious cry of putting an end to strikes by means of arbitration.*"[2]

However, the Parliament of 1905 continued the wage boards, but added to the Act a provision for a court of Industrial Appeals, and the powers and scope of the Act were increased and enlarged. In 1896, six boards were created in four industries: (1) Bakers' Board; (2) Bootmakers' Board; (3) Clothing Manufacturers' Board; (4) Furniture Manufacturers' Board; (5) Shirt Manufacturers' Board; (6) Under-clothing Manufacturers' Board. In the year 1900 alone, a total of twenty-one boards were brought into existence. In 1896, the law was enforced only in Melbourne, the principal city of Victoria, but by 1910, the law had extended its way over the entire state.

An analysis of the machinery of the wage boards will show that the wage-board system was originally based on the principle of conciliation, but that in its present stage compulsory arbitration has been introduced as a final resort. A wage board may be established when requested either by employers or by employees. Both parties forming the wage board have equal representation. The members of the board must not be less than four in number, nor more than ten. They must have been bona-fide employers or employees for at least six months within the three years previous to their appointment. They must have familiarized themselves

[1] Victoria Employers' Federation, *Compulsory Arbitration, A Case Against Them*, p. 11.

[2] *Ibid.*, italics in original.

with the trade which they represent, and for that reason they have been characterized as "a jury of trade experts." Their term of appointment is for three years, but they are eligible for reappointment. The Minister of Interior is required to publish in the *Government Gazette,* before their appointment to a board, the names of the nominees with specification as to the parties they will represent. If within twenty-one days after the date of the publication, one-fifth of the employers or of the adult employees of the trade which will be subject to the Board's award raise objection to the nominees as their representatives, then either the Governor in Council will directly appoint representatives, or the parties about to form the special board may elect again their respective representatives.

The chairman of a special board, as provided by the law, must be impartial. Within fourteen days after their appointment, the members of a board shall nominate a chairman who shall not be one of the members. In case of failure to agree, the Governor in Council has the right to appoint a chairman for the board without nomination from the members.

The powers of a special board fall into five main lines, namely: (1) the fixing of a minimum wage, (2) the establishment of a maximum number of hours, (3) the determination of a special rate of wages for infirm or slow workers, (4) the right to require evidence, and (5) the enforcement of awards. A special board shall determine the lowest price or rates of payment payable to any person or classes of persons employed in the trade in which the board exists. In fixing the lowest rate of wages, the board shall take into consideration:

(1) The nature, kind and class of the work.
(2) The mode and manner in which the work is to be done.

(3) The age and sex of the workers.
(4) The place or locality where the work is to be done.
(5) The hour of the day or night when the work is to be done.
(6) Whether more than six consecutive days' work is to be done.
(7) Whether the work is casual as defined by the Board.
(8) Any recognized usage or custom in the manner of carrying out the work.
(9) Any matter whatsoever which may from time to time be prescribed.[1]

The other functions of the board are comparatively simple. With regard to the matter of hours, the Victorian law specifies that every special board when fixing the lowest wages to be paid to any person or class of persons shall also determine the maximum number of hours per week for which such lowest wages should be payable "according to the nature or conditions of his work." The board is given power to fix lower wages for "infirm or slow workers," wherever it appears to the board that such arrangement is justifiable. In securing evidence, the board can require a person to testify under oath, but there is no provision for the production of books or papers as evidence of one form or other. However, penalty is provided for violation of the determination of the special board. Any person who is guilty of an offense against this law may be penalized for the first offense with a fine of not more than ten pounds, for the second offense, of not more than twenty-five pounds, and for the third or any subsequent offense, of not more than one hundred pounds.

The determination of the board, although it is enforceable, can be changed or challenged in three ways: First, the Governor in Council may at any time suspend the operation of the award of any special board. Such suspension may

[1] Act 1910, no. 2305, sec. 5.

occur when there is a strike threatened in case the determination goes into effect, or whenever the Governor believes that a reconsideration of the case is necessary. Secondly, the validity of the determination of any special board may be challenged by appeal to the Supreme Court. It is then the duty of the Supreme Court to require the Chief Inspector to show cause to prove the legality and validity of the board's action. Thirdly, any dissatisfaction with the determination of a special board, may be brought up to the Court of Industrial Appeal, but all appeals against the awards of a special board must be referred to the Court of Industrial Appeal by the Minister of Labor.

The Court of Industrial Appeal consists of a registrar and of a judge. The registrar is appointed by the Governor in Council and the judge is elected from the judges of the Supreme Court by the judges of this court themselves. The Court may confirm or alter the decision as it sees fit. It possesses all the powers of the Supreme Court, and may exercise in addition all the powers conferred on a special board. It may summon witnesses and require the production of documents and books, but no evidence relating to trade secrets or to the financial position of any party or witness shall be disclosed without the consent of the party or person in question. No barrister or solicitor is allowed to appear before the court, except upon the direction of the court and with the consent of both parties to a dispute. The determination of the court is final, although when satisfied "upon affidavit that a prima facie case for review exists," [1] the court may direct a rehearing. The court, upon the application of the representatives either of the employers or of the employees on the special board, may revise or alter its own determination at any time and from time to time.

[1] Act 1905, no. 1975, sec. 123(9).

The result of the wage-board system can be summarized by answering two questions: first, what has the system accomplished for labor? and secondly, has the system encouraged or checked the growth of industries?

In regard to the first question, the system has brought about some measures which are beneficial to labor. It has eliminated sweating. Every worker in the state receives at least a minimum wage. Conditions and hours of labor also have been improved. It has sometimes been alleged that representatives of employees have been discharged because of their loyalty to their fellow-workers in their negotiations with employers. Undoubtedly there are cases of this sort, but this charge is not easily proved. The round table discussion is beneficial to labor for the simple reason that grievances can easily be brought to the employers' attention.

On the other hand, there are charges against the wage board system from the standpoint of the workers. The annual average amount of wages paid per employee is lower in Victoria and Tasmania, where the wage-board system prevails, than in the other Australian states, where compulsory arbitration exists. In 1910, the annual average amount of salaries and wages paid in pounds per employee in Victoria was £78.18; in Tasmania, £78.81; in New South Wales £90.83; in Queensland, £86.79; in South Australia, £90.44; and in Western Australia, £123.93. In 1913, it was £94.74 in Victoria, £95.18 in Tasmania, but £109.66 in New South Wales, £100.05 in Queensland, £111.66 in South Australia, and £132.31 in Western Australia. In 1923, it was £175.79 in Victoria, £167.23 in Tasmania, but £184.44 in New South Wales, £100.05 in Queensland, £111.66 in South Australia, and £189.32 in Western Australia.[1] Thus, so far as the statistical evidence is concerned, the burden of proof rests upon the supporters of the system.

[1] *Australian Statistics, Quarterly Summary*, Bulletin no. 79, 1920, p. 15, and Bulletin no. 98, Dec., 1924, p. 15.

Although it would be too sweeping a charge against the wage-board system, if the responsibility for the comparatively lower annual average wages were laid entirely upon it, yet this charge cannot be refuted on the ground that Victoria and Tasmania are pastoral and agricultural states. With the possible exception of New South Wales, the industrial development of the other Australian states has not surpassed that of Victoria. Nor can it be refuted on the ground that lower wages may be compensated by shorter hours. The average weekly hours of labor for adult males in all industries, except shipping, grazing and agriculture, in December, 1923 was 47.06 in Victoria, 47.27 in Tasmania, but 46.73 in New South Wales, 45.51 in Queensland, 47.00 in South Australia and 46.66 in Western Australia.[1] Again the average weekly hours for adult females of the same period for all industries was 46.13 in Victoria, 47.86 in Tasmania, but 45.81 in New South Wales, 45.60 in Queensland. 46.10 in South Australia and 45.97 in Western Australia.[2] It is only fair to conclude then, with due respect to the beneficial aspects of the system, that the institution which is in duty bound to make adjustments must share at least partly the responsibility for the slow advance made in the matter of wages and for the tardy reduction in hours.

With respect to the second question, namely, the relation between the operation of the wage-board system and the growth of industries in the states in which the system exists, it is safe to say that the industrial progress in Victoria warrants a positive conclusion that the system has not retarded the industrial development of the state. In 1896, when the wage board system first came into operation, there were in Victoria 3,370 factories with 40,814 workers. By 1910

[1] Commonwealth Bureau of Census and Statistics, *Labour Report*, no. 14, 1923, p. 68.

[2] *Ibid.*, p. 69.

there were in the same state 5,362 factories with 83,053 workers. In 1920, the number of factories reached the mark of 6,038 and the number of workers 136,522, and in 1923, there were 7,096 factories and 152,625 workers. This growth in manufacturing industries is as great as any that has taken place in other countries.

III. COMPULSORY ARBITRATION IN NEW SOUTH WALES

The development of government intervention in disputes between capital and labor in New South Wales began, as in New Zealand and elsewhere, in the nineties. The workingmen of New Zealand, after the maritime strike in 1890, succeeded in their agitation for government arbitration in the passage of the Act of 1894. A similar movement on the part of the New South Wales workers was inaugurated at the same time. As a result, in 1892, the " Trade Dispute Conciliation and Arbitration Act " was passed. This Act was to remain in operation for four years, but owing to the lack of enforcement, the Act failed to bring about the adjustment that had been anticipated. The reason was that employers generally refused to send representatives to the "Conciliation Councils." Consequently, before the expiration of the four-year term, the system had collapsed.

Since the attempt at conciliation had proved a failure, New South Wales, in 1901, took a radical step to compel agreement by the adoption of compulsory arbitration. The law of 1901 was founded on the New Zealand model of 1894, but the section in the latter which provided for conciliation boards was entirely struck out. Other provisions of the New South Wales Law resembled very closely those of the New Zealand Law. This Act, however, also failed in its operation.

The failure of this second experiment were traceable to two causes:—the congestion of cases in the Industrial Court, causing delay and discontent, and the inability of the Court to exercise its jurisdiction as it was expected to.

The congestion was the result of many causes. The omission of the conciliation boards and the manner in which the unions brought their disputes to the Court were important causes. Had the Act retained the conciliation boards, a number of small disputes might have been adjusted, but instead of adopting the method of weeding out small differences, the Court had to assume the task of hearing every dispute, great or small. At the same time, the unions regarded the arbitration machinery as a means for securing industrial regulations, and consequently, whenever disputes arose, whether acute or not, the unions referred them to the Court and expected redress of grievances. As a result the Court could not by any effort hew its way through the jungle of work which had sprung up all around it.[1]

Again, there was another peculiar obstacle, which existed only in New South Wales, and that was the concentration of the mining industry in the region. A large portion of the Court's time was consumed by the disputes arising in that industry. During the first year of its work, the Court sat for only eighty-one days, of which one colliery dispute, the Illawarra case, occupied thirty-two days. Congestion, therefore, was in sight from the very beginning. In the following year agitation was started for a special Court for the mining industry, and in 1903, a bill for this purpose was introduced, but it failed to pass the House. Another bill was again introduced in the Legislative Council, in the following year, but it too was rejected. Similar proposals in the three years subsequent to the latter defeat gained no favor from the unsympathetic Parliament.

Another cause of congestion in the Court's proceedings arose from some accidental events coupled with the ineffi-

[1] New South Wales, *Parliamentary Papers*, vol. i, p. xxv, 1913.

ciency of the Wade Administration. In 1904, a month and a week were lost owing to the illness of certain members of the Court. In 1905, from May to August, a period of three months, the Court was absolutely idle, on account of Justice Cohen's resignation and the failure or neglect of the government to appoint a successor.[1] So the record of vacation and illness continued as time went on, and at the conclusion of the six years of the Act's operation, nine months were wasted through these accidental causes.

The second major reason for the failure of the Act was a decision of the "Higher Court", greatly limiting the jurisdiction of the Industrial Court. The leading case in this connection was the controversy between the Colliery Employees' Federation and Messrs. Brown.[2] This case dated back to a dispute which arose between the parties in 1903 on some conditions of employment. After a long delay, the union filed a new claim, including also the original claim, before the Arbitration Court. But the summons were neglected according to the usual practice of the Arbitration Court at the time. On June 15, 1905, all the miners involved in the dispute declared a walkout without sending any notice to the employer. The matter was brought to the State Supreme Court which declared that in spite of the fact that this was an industrial matter between employers and employees, "the union did not come into it at all."[3] The State Supreme Court justified Brown's contention that when the men ceased work, pending a settlement of dispute, the Arbitration Court had no power to entertain the suit. Furthermore, it maintained that it was a dangerous policy to allow officers of the union to raise disputes over the heads

[1] New South Wales, *Parliamentary Debates*, March 19, 1908, p. 319.

[2] New South Wales, *Arbitration Report*, 1905, pp. 294-299.

[3] *Ibid.*, p. 297 (Hereafter *A. R.* stands for *Arbitration Report*).

of the employees and call upon the employers to appear before the Court to settle disputes which the employees did not desire to raise.

The matter was finally referred to the "Higher Court" for review.[1] This Court unanimously upheld the decision of the State Court and declared that the object of the Act was to establish a tribunal for the determination of industrial disputes. It was "not to constitute a board of trade, or a municipal body with power to make by-laws to regulate trade, but a Court of Arbitration, for hearing and determining industrial disputes, and matters referred to it."[2]

After this famous decision, the hands of the Arbitration Court were definitely tied. The Higher Court had laid down two principles, namely, first that an industrial union of employees could not carry on an industrial dispute with an employer who had none of its members in his employ, and secondly, that in order to have jurisdiction over any case, the Arbitration Court should satisfy itself of the existence of a dispute between the employer and his own employees. These two principles put the Arbitration Court in a legal tangle from which it could not extricate itself, though it was allowed to struggle on. Justice Heydon, President of the Arbitration Court, complaining of the situation, declared in a later decision[3] that the bark of the Industrial Arbitration Act had made a brave show with sails outspread when directed by his predecessor, but that since he took the helm, "the Act has been riddled; shell broken fore and aft, and reduced to a sinking hulk. No pilot could navigate such a craft. Do not say, however, that no ship can sail the seas, because this one has been so badly built."

[1] *Commonwealth Law Report*, vol. iii, p. 255; also 1906 *A. R.*, pp. 71-76.

[2] 1906 *A. R.*, p. 74.

[3] Amalgamated Miners' Association *v.* Great Cobar, Limited, 1907, *A. R.*, 59.

As a result of the Brown decision, many cases on the list for hearing in the Arbitration Court had to be struck out, because they had been based on disputes between employers and the union. This cast a huge shadow of disappointment over the prospects of the labor unions which had been waiting for months for the adjustment of their claims. The Wade Administration had to shoulder the blame for the industrial unrest which occurred subsequently. The radical wing of the union leaders agitated for the abolition of industrial arbitration and advocated direct action in the form of a revolutionary general strike. Partly because of general discontent among the working classes, re-echoed by the press and other agencies of public opinion, and partly because the Act expired in June, 1908, a new arbitration act was passed in April, 1908.

The new legislation of 1908 consisted of the principal act and an amendment enacted in the same year. The law, including other innovations, made two changes, namely, the jurisdiction of the Court embraced all industrial matters whether disputes existed or not, and the machinery of conciliation was fused with that of compulsory arbitration.

According to the judicial interpretation of the former Act of 1901, any matter referred to the Arbitration Court had to be a dispute, or at least a "paper dispute", in order to give the Court jurisdiction. The Act under consideration sought to widen the Court's power and remove an alleged pregnant cause of delay. Strange to say, however, the latter Act was entitled "The Industrial Dispute Act", while the repealed Act had been called "Industrial Arbitration Act." Even in the amendment of the same year the same title remained unchanged. On the other hand, according to the Act of 1908, industrial disputes received a broad definition. It defined an industrial dispute to be any controversy in relation to industrial matters originating between an employer or industrial union of employers on the one hand, and an industrial union of employees or trade union or branch or not less than twenty employees on the other hand. The individual laborer was no longer a party to a dispute, for the union assumed the responsibility of defending the interests of its members and every worker was expected to join the union and bargain collectively through the union.

The next important innovation was the fusion of the wage-board system with compulsory arbitration, which caused hot debates in Parliament. The administration maintained that the adoption of the wage-board system would prevent congestion of cases in the Arbitration Court and also that it would safeguard the principle of free competition. Premier Wade was of the opinion that the congestion of cases was due to the administration of the Court with regard to the preference clause that the Court had to decide whether or not union preference should be granted. He thought that the congestion of cases would be removed by the adoption of the wage board system, and that if employers were willing to give union preference it was their own bargain, but that Parliament should not impose this condition upon them. He did not oppose in clear terms, however, the vesting of this power of granting union preference in the Arbitration Court. He proposed that the wage boards should have full power to settle the question of preference, but that Parliament should not adopt a provision forcing unwilling employers to employ union men.[1]

While a law compelling union preference was too great an aspiration to be brought to realization at the time, the leaders of the labor group in Parliament objected to the wage-board system not because it did not guarantee union preference but because it failed to protect labor representatives on the boards. They held that even though the Law

[1] New South Wales, *Parliamentary Debates*, March 19, 1908, p. 308.

did not permit the employer to discharge the labor representatives on a board, he could blacklist the men who fought for their fellow-employees.

As a result of this objection that the wage-board system was defective because the representatives of the employees ran the risk of being discharged and were without any protection against this danger, the provisions of the Bill concerning wage boards were greatly modified. Conciliation existed in name, but compulsory arbitration was the reality. The Act provided that a board, besides its chairman, should consist of not more than ten members equally representing employers and employees. The chairman of a board was to be appointed by the Governor, upon the nomination of the Industrial Court, provided that if the parties should agree upon a chairman, the Arbitration Court shoud nominate the person so elected to be the chairman. The board or any two or more members thereof, when authorized by the board under the hand of its chairman, might enter and inspect any premises used in any industry. "If any person hinders or obstructs a board or any member thereof in the exercise of the powers conferred by the section, he shall be liable to a penalty not exceeding ten pounds." Moreover, the board might require the production of evidence "as in good conscience it thinks to be the best available whether strictly legal evidence or not." The board was further empowered to summon witnesses. So the board exercised practically all the powers which the Arbitration Court possessed.

The original intention of the Premier in introducing the Bill was to bring about round-table discussion. When the House debated on the amendment of the Law in November, 1908, Premier Wade asserted that in the Principal Act "the Government made the innovation of doing away with the constitution of the old arbitration court and introducing a system that had been proved to be successful in Victoria for a number of years past." [1] The alleged advantage was that under the wage-board system, the personnel of the boards was increased to as high as ten or more and as they represented only the parties, the necessity for calling for detailed evidence was largely removed. Therefore, the adoption of the method of taking evidence in preference to the conversational methods of adjustment, came as a great disappointment to the government. The Premier complained that the boards "were apparently wedded to the old system in which they had been trained in New South Wales, and began their proceedings by taking evidence in great detail and at great length."

The Act met objections also from both employers and employees. The former complained that the Act was responsible for bringing 270 boards into existence, and that the employers who found themselves under the jurisdiction of so many different boards had suffered great losses of time and expense in attending conferences. The latter voiced their disappointment that the Act failed to bring about speedy settlement. The reasons for this phenomenon were not difficult to comprehend. The Act failed to classify industries, and as a result, a multiplicity of boards sprang up having overlapping jurisdiction. A number of similar disputes, which might have been settled by one board, were brought before several boards. This meant an increase in the number of disputes. But what aggravated the situation still more was the limited number of persons in the community who were qualified and willing to act as chairmen of the boards. The limited number of judges and lawyers available for meeting the great demand was too apparent, and even those upon whom the parties might agree, could not always be persuaded to serve. Moreover, the sittings had, as a rule, to take place at night, when the chairmen

[1] New South Wales, *Parliamentary Debates*, Nov. 25, 1908, p. 2803.

could afford the time. Similar considerations also applied to the personal convenience of the members of the board Consequently, the work of the boards could not be carried on with the rapidity and satisfaction desired by the parties concerned.

The Act struggled on. In 1911, a labor government came into power. George Stephenson Beeby, Minister of Labor, introduced a bill which afterward became law in April 1912. This law repealed the Act of 1908 and re-established the Act of 1901 with some radical changes. In the matter of registration of industrial unions and with regard to the jurisdiction conferred upon the boards, the provisions of this law resembled those of the New Zealand acts. Nevertheless, in many respects it has its own distinguishing features.

1. As a proposed remedy for defects in the existing law, the Act of 1912 adopts a logical classification of industries, grouping the numerous crafts under a few industries set off in a schedule. It reduces the different industries into twenty-seven groups, and sets up a board for each of these groups. New boards can only be constituted by the Minister of Labor and Industries upon the proclamation of the Governor. Each of the boards created is presided over by a chairman appointed by the Minister of Labor and Industries upon the recommendation of the Industrial Court. Besides its chairman, a board consists of two or four members equally representing employers and employees in the specified industry. An exception to this provision is made for industries employing largely females. In industries of this nature members of the boards may be persons from outside the industries.

2. Another significant feature of the law is the combination into one system of the machinery for conciliation and mediation as well as investigation and arbitration. The act

provides for district mediation. The State is divided into three "colliery districts", the northern, southern and western districts. In each of these districts a so-called "conciliation committee" exists. A "conciliation committee", besides its chairman, consists of two or four members representing employers on the one hand and employees on the other. Unanimous agreement is a necessary requirement for the election of the chairman. In case of deadlock, the Governor shall make the appointment. The chief function of these committees is to keep in touch with the industrial situation of the State and to mediate at an early stage any industrial dispute which may arise. The jurisdiction of these committees, however, does not extend to non-registered unions.

In close connection with the conciliation committees, there is a "special commissioner", who "may require the attendance of any persons to meet in conference whenever any question has arisen." [1] He may compel the contending parties to attend a conference, when, in his opinion, a dispute might lead to a strike or lockout, when "either no board has been constituted which would have jurisdiction in the matter or temporary agreement should be made before the matter is submitted to a board." [1] By this measure, the Act aims to reach both the registered unions and the non-registered unions, so far as mediation is concerned.

In the matters of investigation and arbitration, the industrial boards and the Arbitration Court exercise wide powers, determine the number of working hours, and grant union preference. By giving the boards the right to decide on the issue of preference and by making the Court the final arbitrator in the matter, the Act has conferred upon these tribunals the widest power that it is within its capacity to exercise.

[1] Section 43.

3. Finally, the Act establishes a new method for the enforcement of awards by imposing fines on wages. It abandons the usual enforcement by imprisonment in case of unlawful strike or lockout. It provides that any employer who causes or participates in an unlawful lockout, shall be punished by a fine not exceeding one thousand pounds and that any employee who participates in an unlawful strike, shall be ordered to pay a penalty not exceeding fifty pounds. The fine upon the employee, if not paid, is collected by deduction from the wages of the employee as a first charge. The Court may collect the sum from the old or new employer of the employee who is guilty of the offense, until the full amount is paid.

The Act has been subjected to constant changes, adapting it to the persistent economic changes of the country. All the innovations, which have been so far adopted, however, have wrought no serious change in principle, but rather have widened or limited the jurisdiction of the law in one phase or other and also attempted to improve the efficiency of the Court. The Act was amended for the first time in 1916, then it was twice amended in 1918 and again in 1919, 1920 and 1922.

The significant alteration of the law in 1916 was the provision increasing the number of judges to three and empowering them to have two or more sittings at the same time. The question of efficiency presents itself in no obscure manner and requires no further explanation. The principle of economy, however, also came into play. The amendment was defended as a measure for economy. At the second reading of the bill, the Minister of Labor and Industries asserted that the addition of another judge to the Industrial Court aimed at the abolition of the industrial boards. The board system at the time cost £19,000 per annum, while the expenditure for the salary of the extra judges, including incidental expenses, amounted only to £3,500. The bill, however, contained no provision for the abolition of the boards, though the government expressed this intention in Parliament.

Representatives of employers called the bill "desirable and necessary reform", because the employing classes at this time regarded the industrial board system as a burden falling unduly upon them. There were boards having jurisdiction in several lines of business, and it was a physical impossibility for a manager to attend to all his required duties. For this reason, a member of the Legislative Council, though he might have spoken too strongly, charged the existing law with having put not only property but human life in jeopardy, meaning that the lives of employers were endangered.

The next amendment came in 1918, which aimed chiefly at a more rigid regulation of union activities. Strikes are illegal in government service. Under no circumstance can the employees lawfully declare a strike against "the Crown" or any minister, trust, commission or board exercising executive or administrative functions on behalf of the government of the state or municipalities. A heavy penalty of five hundred pounds is imposed upon the union whose members take part in an illegal strike of this nature. "Where any trade union fails within the time prescribed by the court to pay any penalty imposed by the Court, the trade union shall be wound up,"[1] and the Court shall appoint a receiver of its assets to pay the penalty due to the government. Moreover, a proprietor and publisher of any newspaper which advises or instigates an illegal strike shall for each offence be liable to a penalty not exceeding one hundred pounds.[2]

[1] Section 17.

[2] Section 15.

Two other significant provisions of the amendment of 1918 are: (1) the limitation of the powers of the boards and the Court in fixing wages for government employees; (2) the creation of the Board of Trade. The Act declares that the industrial boards and the Arbitration Court have no power to fix the wages of government employees. At the same time the Act created the Board of Trade whose function is to make public investigation as to the increase or decrease in the cost of living and to fix a living wage for every district of the state.

The act was assented to during the War when patriotism generally turned against labor. Unquestionably, this legislation was aimed at the unions, with a view to prohibiting strikes. The conservative Government, under the leadership of Premier William Arthur Holman, bitterly attacked the unions for the betrayal of the cause of arbitration. The government took this attitude because of the strikes which had occurred in the previous years. Since the War, the workers had launched the "one big union" program. The Premier charged this program as being a "sign of degeneration and growing intellectual and moral weakness" in the labor movement, when the union "repudiates appeals to justice." Labor leaders, on the other hand, denounced the Act as being unfair to labor in view of the severe penalties imposed on the employees. They held that it was impossible to prove a lockout against an employer.

After the important changes through the amendment of 1918, the later amendments made no significant change in the existing machinery, except to add clauses concerning the basic wage. The Act of 1919 provides that whenever a declaration as to the living wage is made, the Court may vary the wage provisions contained in an industrial agreement. The Act of 1920 declares that an employee in order to be entitled to the basic wage must perform a minimum of twenty-one hours of work per week. Finally, the Amendment of 1922 deals also with the question of fixing a living wage. This time the law concerns itself with the intervals between changes in the rate of the living wage. The Act requires, in well defined language, that the Board of Trade fix a living wage at such times as the Board may think fit, but at intervals of not less than three months and only after a public inquiry into the increase or decrease in the cost of living.

The last amendment was a result of the discontent on the part of wage earners on account of a wage reduction which occurred in the same year. The amendment of 1918 brought the Board of Trade into being and vested it with power to fix a living wage. The weekly living wages for adult males in 1918, 1919, 1920 and 1921 were respectively £3 (for Sydney and Suburbs), £3 17s (also for Sydney and Suburbs), £4 5s (for the State, excluding Newcastle, South Coast and Central Tablelands Areas), and £4 2s (for the State excluding County of Yoncowinna).[1] In 1922, a reduction of 7s per week occurred. This reduction caused loud condemnation of the government by the labor leaders in Parliament. They attacked the administration of the Board of Trade for its acceptance of the Commonwealth statistician's report without making an independent investigation, on the ground that local matters require independent adjustments. The Court was also blamed for its indorsement of the reduction based on statistics from the same source. The amendment, therefore, requires the Board of Trade to make independent investigations and fix a living wage whenever the evidence proves its necessity.

The entire history of the New South Wales experiment may be summarized by calling to mind once more the mile

[1] New South Wales Board of Trade, *Compendium of Living Wage Declaration and Report*, 1922.

stones which mark the development of the system. New South Wales took its first progressive step toward compulsory arbitration in 1901. In the decade prior to that date, New South Wales had suffered a profound depression in the labor market. The Act gained its accession to the statute book chiefly because of the tremendous pressure brought to bear by the Labor Party demanding arbitral determination.

The next move occurred in 1908, when the industrial development of the country produced disputes of greater complexity which rendered the weakness of the provision for a single tribunal apparent. Grievances went unredressed, on account of the congestion of cases in the Arbitration Court. Again, the discontented army of workers, with the help of their sympathizing friends, returned the Labor Party to power in 1911. Then the amendment of 1912 came out in the pristine freshness of the Labor Government. Improvements in this principal act were assented to in 1916, 1918, 1919, 1920 and 1922. The most significant of these amendments has been that of 1918 which created the Board of Trade to inquire into the matter of the living wage.

The result of the experiment is difficult to summarize in a few paragraphs. An analysis of some adequate answers to two major question should be sufficient for the present purpose. These questions are: First, to what extent has the system brought about industrial peace? Second, how far has the operation of compulsory arbitration affected the freedom of contract?

The answer to the first question is mainly statistical. From 1913 to 1923, New South Wales has witnessed 3104 industrial disputes resulting in suspensions of work and business. While a large majority of the cases were settled by compulsory arbitration or compulsory conferences, the machinery failed to affect adjustment in many cases. Among the 3104 disputes, in 99 cases the strikes were brought to a close by filling the places of the workers.

Some members of the Legislative Council charge that "arbitration is about the greatest failure" in the State. "We did hope that it would make for the settlement of disputes and abolish strikes, but the law as it stands, has resulted in the multiplication of disputes and strikes." [1] It is unfair to take this attitude towards the Law. Industrial disputes originate not only from the machinery set up for their adjustment, but also from the discontent fostered by unsatisfactory hours, wages and working conditions. True, the inefficiency of the tribunal for adjustment may have increased the discontent, but that is not the major cause, and the addition of two more judges has greatly relieved the situation.

It would be equally unfair to ridicule the State of New South Wales as a champion of industrial legislation because it suffers a greater number of industrial upheavals than other states. The difference in the types of occupation prevailing in the different states accounts for the disproportion in the number of disputes. The majority of the disputes which occurred in New South Wales came from the mining industry. Thus in 1923, which recorded the lowest number of industrial disputes in New South Wales since the beginning of the World War, out of a total of 200 cases, 157 occurred in the mining industry, while in the same year, there existed in Victoria 3 cases and in Queenland only 8 cases. However, the question must be definitely answered: that compulsory arbitration in New South Wales, as elsewhere, has not succeeded in preventing industrial war.

The next question which concerns the operation of the system is the effect of the law with respect to the freedom of contract. This includes chiefly the question of employ-

[1] New South Wales, *Parliamentary Debates*, December 12, 1916, p 3475.

ment and dismissal. The law has conferred on the Court the power to fix hours and wages. The effect of this provision is self-evident, because it indicates so clearly that the employer's right of fixing wages and hours has been abrogated. The effects of the law on the rights of employment and discharge, however, require some detailed discussion.

The question of employment, for the present purpose, may be crystalized into one principal issue, that of union preference. There are three types of union preference in New South Wales, namely, ***mandatory preference, statutory preference*** and ***obligatory preference***.[1] By mandatory preference is meant the preference given to unionists since 1912 in an order handed down by the Commonwealth Government which required in all contracts of employment the insertion of these words: "All things being equal, absolute preference is to be given to unionists in the employment of workmen for all work carried on under this contract." Statutory preference, on the other hand, results from an enactment passed by the state Parliament empowering the Court of Arbitration to grant preference to the unionists. The Act of 1901 directed that "between members of an industrial union of employees and other persons, offering their labor at the same time, such members be employed in preference to such other persons, other things being equal. . . ."[2] The law of 1908 repealed this provision, but the Act of 1912 reintroduced it.[3] The third type of

[1] Mr. A. B. Piddington, in his *Final Report of the Royal Commission on Industrial Arbitration in the State of New South Wales, Parliamentary Papers*, vol. i, 1913, proposed the following terms: absolute preference, normal preference and effective preference which, in my opinion, are misleading for the reason that these terms fail to define the real nature of the types. The credit for originating the classification, however, belongs to him.

[2] Section 36 (f).

[3] Section 24 (g).

union preference is obligatory preference[1] which declares that in cases where the Court has granted preference to the unionists, the employer should fulfill the obligation by giving the union notice beforehand informing the union of the amount of work to be done and the number of men required. The following discussion deals chiefly with the second type, because it reveals the policy of the Court in regard to this matter.

The question of union preference has been the most important issue in the continuous struggle between capital and labor in New South Wales. Parliament has conferred upon the Court the power to grant union preference at its discretion, but has not laid down well defined conditions as to the circumstances under which the Court should exercise this power. In the course of adjudication, and undoubtedly many a time with great embarrassment, the Court has formulated rules for its practice, changing them at times when the change of industrial conditions warranted the alteration. The entire course of adjudication concerning union preference, up to the present time, has been guided by five principles: (1) *the principle of obedience and encouragement,* (2) *the principle of judgment by result,* (3) *the principle of neutrality,* (4) *the principle of majority,* and (5) *the principle of good faith.*

1. When the Court first attacked the question of granting or refusing union preference, it had to find some ground for the justification of its action. It was only natural that the Court first took the principle of obedience and encouragement. Under the New South Wales system of compulsory arbitration, the machinery would be completely idle if the unions refused to register. One of the purposes of the

[1] The "Higher Court" declared obligatory preference *ultra vires* of the Arbitration Court in the Trolley Draymen's case 2, *C. L. R.*, p. 509 (1905).

system in its early stages was the encouragement of the formation of unions, for the cardinal principle of arbitration was collective bargaining, and collective bargaining, so far as the employees were concerned, necessitated the formation of unions, through which the law might function. The industrial unions gave life to and maintained the existence of the act. For this reason, H. E. Cohen, first President Judge of the Arbitration Court, declared in the Trolley Draymen's case, that "finding therein that collective bargaining, or the existence of industrial unions for the purpose of the Act operating, is vital, I consider . . . that preference should be given to unionists." [1] The interpretation of this opinion was that since the union had obeyed the requirements of the Act, preference should be given to the members in order that the Act might function to the fullest extent.

In making the argument that preference should be given to registered unions as an inducement to support the law, Judge Cohen introduced another principle entering into the determination of union preference, when he inserted the clause—"Where the industrial union fairly and practically and substantially represents the industry, so far as the employees are concerned." This is the principle of majority. But in spite of this declaration, it was admitted in the Amalgamated Miners' case,[2] that the union at Broken Hill had not a majority of the employees in its ranks, and yet preference was granted. The principle of obedience and encouragement therefore played a dominant part in determining union preference during the first stage of the development of arbitration.

2. When Charles G. Heydon succeeded Judge Cohen as

[1] Trolley Draymen and Carters' Union v. Master Carriers Association, 1905, *A. R.* 38, p. 45.

[2] Barrier Branch of the Amalgamated Miners' Association v. Broken Hill Propillary Company, Limited, 1903, *A. R.* 525 at p. 534.

President Judge of the Court, he took a conservative stand by relying on the principle of judgment by result. This principle meant that if preference had already been given to unionists by an employer the Court should declare that the custom should be continued. Thus, in the Wharf Laborers' case, the Judge said: "In this position the only principle which I can discover is . . . . that as far as possible the same must be given in the award as would have been arrived at by the parties themselves." The Judge concluded the decision by granting preference and said: "the Casual Wharf Laborers' Union has already won preference for itself, and for a long time past there has been no place on the wharves for any casual laborer not a member of their union."

3. The third principle which served for some years as a safe ground for the Court in granting union preference was that of neutrality. This principle was most frequently used by the Commonwealth Arbitration Court, which declared that the purpose of granting preference was to secure the neutrality of the employers in their employment of labor and not to make discrimination against the unionists. It followed, therefore, that preference should be granted "only when it apeared to the Court to be necessary to restrain an employer from active opposition to the employment of unionists."

4. The principle which has been the most frequently used, even up to the present time, is the rule of majority. In the early stage of the New South Wales experiment, the rule of majority of employees employed had not been a sufficient reason for granting preference. But in later stages of the development of the Court's policy, this principle has played a dominant part. Since the Wire-Mattress case [1] in 1906, the Court has constantly referred to the majority argument in support of its position. In this case the Court declared

[1] *Wire-Mattress Makers' Award*, 1906, *A. R.* 293.

that "only a minority of the workers appear to have joined the union. It seems clear that they could not have enforced preference for themselves; and indeed, in the largest establishment, they seem to have gained no footing at all." [1]

Another important case which reaffirmed the position of the Court with respect to this matter was the Iron and Shipbuilding Trades' case in 1915,[2] in which the Court refused union preference on the sole ground that there was insufficient evidence to prove that the union included a large majority of the employees. The Court maintained its ruling in spite of the report submitted by the secretary of the union, proving that unionists composed the greater part of the number of employees in the trade. It held that the probability was not enough. "There are circumstances which make it seem probable to me [Judge Heydon] that a large majority of these workers are in the union; certainly there is nothing to disprove it; but the probability is not enough, and I must reluctantly hold that there was not sufficient evidence to support the act of the Board." [3]

5. Finally, the last stage of reasoning in support of union preference has been the principle of good faith. In the Shop Assistants' case of 1923, this principle is clearly defined. The Court rules that preference should be granted to the union "that has shown its earnest and sincere desire to satisfactorily carry out and make suitable relations between employer and employee under this Act." [4] According to this principle, union preference has reached its widest interpretation. So long as the union observes the arbitration law and does not violate any of the provisions prohibiting strikes and other unfair practices, it is entitled to the

[1] *Op. cit.*, p. 295.

[2] *Iron and Shipbuilding Trades*, 1915, *A. R.* 270.

[3] *Ibid.* at p. 273.

[4] Shop Assistants' case, 1923 *A. R.* 129, p. 131.

privilege of preference. Undoubtedly, there is a great advantage in this argument, because the Court may use preference as a means to strengthen the enforcement of the Law.

The next issue, which also affects seriously the freedom of contract, is the question concerning the right of dismissal. Under English common law an employer has a right to discharge his employee with or without notice. Compulsory arbitration abrogates this right, not to the extent that dismissal is unlawful, but that discharge without notice is illegal. Furthermore, under the New South Wales system, an employer must not only abstain from terminating a contract without a notice of fourteen days, but also give up his right of terminating a contract as a result of an award. The Act prohibits an employer from dismissing his employee on account of the latter's connection with the union or his rights to the benefit of an award.

Section 52 of the "Act of 1912 to 1920" declares:

> If an employer dismisses from his employment any employee by reason of the fact that the employee is a member of a board, or of a trade union, or an industrial union, or has absented himself from work through being engaged in other duties as member of a board or is entitled to the benefit of an award or of an industrial agreement, the Court may order such employer to pay a penalty not exceeding twenty pounds for each employee so dismissed.

It should be emphasized that this provision under discussion does not annul the employer's right to discharge. It merely provides conditions under which dismissal is unlawful. The difficulty of administering this provision is clearly demonstrated in a recent case in connection with the Federated Pastrycooks' Union.[1] The history of the case began

[1] Federated Pastrycook Employees' Union of Australia, New South Wales Branch *v.* Gartell White Limited, 1924 *A. R.* 5.

when a certain employee, after an employment for some time as assistant and while receiving the same wage, was given the duties previously performed by a pastrycook who had left the company. The employee gave particulars of his duties to an industrial inspector, informing him of the change of his duties without a corresponding advance in his wages. The employer then assigned him his former duties as assistant and then discharged him for giving information to the inspector. The Court held that the man was discharged for giving information to an inspector and not for the reason of receiving the benefit of an award as the union alleged. The employer was not guilty of violation of the Arbitration Act.

In spite of the fact that cases like this tend to show that arbitral decisions are often disadvantageous to employees, compulsory arbitration has benefited the working classes in New South Wales rather than suppressed them. The above analysis justifies this conclusion.

IV. WAGE BOARD ADJUSTMENT AND COMPULSORY ARBITRATION IN QUEENSLAND

Queensland, in the matter of making provision for the adjustment of industrial disputes, has repeated the experience of New South Wales and of Victoria. The Wage Board Act of 1908 grew up as an extension of the Factories and Shops Act of 1900. The organization of the wage boards bore marked resemblances to the Victoria system. Each consisted of an equal number of representatives of employers and employees together with a chairman to be nominated by them and to be appointed by the Governor in Council. The members of any wage board, excluding the chairman, should not be less than four, nor more than twelve.

The wage board has two chief duties—the fixing of the

rate of wages and of the hours of labor. In the matter of fixing wages, the board may determine a living wage for any person or class of persons in any factory within its jurisdiction. It can go into such minute details as determining the time and place for payment of piece wages, the extra wage due for work done at a particular time of the day or particular season of the year, and many other factors. With respect to the question of hours of work, the board can also act in an equally detailed fashion. It can determine the amount of "waiting time" necessary in piecework; it can fix the duration of time allowed for meals and the maximum length of the working day for any employee in the state, etc.

The enactment of this law came about as a result of agitation by the labor party. Previous to its enactment, the bill was passed twice by the Legislative Assembly, once in 1906 and again in 1907, but it was twice rejected by the Legislative Council. Finally in 1908, when the labor party brought the pressure of public opinion to bear upon the upper body of the Legislature, the bill became a law without even a minor alteration. Following the passage of the Act, wages rose and hours began gradually to diminish. While the employers were still reluctant to surrender much of their private rights in the conducting of their business, the workers continued their agitation for further improvements in their lot by a persistent attempt to secure stronger unions.

A significant event came about in 1912, when the Brisbane Tramway Company refused to allow its employees to wear union badges and dismissed a number of those who had done so. The motive of the company's refusal was to prevent the spread of unionism by eliminating union activities and publicity. The union declared a strike as a protest against the company. Subsequently, a general strike followed. Special constables were enrolled but without avail. The strike resulted in the collapse of the campaign of the workers. While bitter hostility towards unionism was burning in the hearts of most business men and capitalists, the Industrial Peace Act of 1912 was framed and passed.

This act provided, for the first time, in the State of Queensland, for an industrial court. The Industrial Court was to be composed of two judges. A judge or acting judge sitting alone should constitute the Court, which was to hear all the appeals from the industrial boards. The organization and nature of the industrial boards remained practically the same as they were under the wage-board system.

Two significant features of the Act were the sections dealing with strikes and lockouts and the provision for refusing union preference. The Act declared that all strikes and lockouts were illegal unless a fourteen days' notice had been given to the registrar of the industrial board to the effect that a secret ballot had been conducted among the employers or employees, as the case might be, in the industry concerned favoring the action thus taken. A labor union or an employers' association could be represented in the Industrial Court, or in an industrial board, by its member, or officer or authorized agent, but no party should be represented by counsel or solicitor or salaried officer of any industrial or other labor union or employers' association, or by any member of Parliament. The second feature of the Act is that it specifically declared that there should be no discrimination against anyone on account of his membership or non-membership in a union. This section aimed to put an end to the controversy over union preference. The prohibition of the representation of a party in proceedings before the Court or the boards was an attempt to eliminate political influence on industrial matters. The refusal of union preference was also an attempt to divorce politics from industry by preventing union leaders from becoming political bosses.

In 1915, however, a labor government came into power and a bill was introduced repealing the Industrial Peace Act of 1912, and putting in its place an act, the outstanding feature of which, was the provision empowering the Industrial Court to grant union preference as it was in practice in New South Wales. This clause led to the rejection of the bill, and in the following year the bill was passed without the preference clause. When the Court came to interpret the law, it exercised the power of granting preference since the Court was not restricted in making its decisions by the proceedings of parliamentary discussions. The absence of the union preference clause has not, therefore, changed the character of the Act. Moreover, the Act of 1916 contains many liberal provisions. The forty-eight-hour week was definitely established by law. The principle of equal pay for equal work was also adopted. Work which resulted in equal return of profit to the employer, was to be entitled to equal pay regardless of sex.

In operation, therefore, the Law of 1916 follows closely the system existing in New South Wales. The organization of the Queensland system consists of three bodies: the "Court of Industrial Arbitration", the "Industrial Boards", and the "Conciliation Committees". The Court which consists of two or three judges, is deemed a branch of the Supreme Court and every judge of the Court of Industrial Arbitration has the status of a judge of the Supreme Court. The organization of the other two bodies, namely, the Industrial Boards and the Conciliation Committees, show no marked differences. The only difference lies in the jurisdiction of these two bodies. An industrial board undertakes to make recommendations for one or more industries, while a conciliation committee confines its functions of conciliation to one or more industries within a particular district. The chief function of the Industrial Boards is to coordinate the work of the conciliation committees and to deal with adjustments within an industry regardless of geographic limitations.

A few changes have occurred since 1916, but the organization of the system remains unaltered. The amendment of 1923 inserted some minor changes into the Act with respect to registration, while the last amendment which was added in 1924, reduced the working week from forty-eight hours to forty-four hours.

The general reactions towards the system present some phenomena of great significance. Before the inauguration of the wage-board law in 1908, labor leaders agitated for such machinery, but employers were either indifferent towards it or strongly opposed to it. After the span of but a few years, during which employers came to learn that the wage-board system could accomplish desirable results, the president of the Queensland Employers' Federation in his annual address expressed the opinion that wage boards were "the most practical means" of dealing with industrial differences, because both the employers and the employees were acquainted with the practical working of the business in which the dispute took place. He went so far as to advocate the adoption of compulsory arbitration in the event that wage boards should prove unsatisfactory.

In 1912 compulsory arbitration was actually added to the Queensland statute book. In that year Queensland employers saw the spectre of industrial upheaval. They aimed their legislative weapon at the monster and hoped that the source of evil would be removed by outlawing the privilege of preference to the union giant. Unfortunately, for the employers, the union giant could not be subdued. It became more formidable. The Labor Government came into power. In the following year, the Law of 1916 was passed. Since the enactment of this law the Court possesses the power to grant union preference as it sees fit and justifiable.

With this change in the arbitration law, the employers completely altered their attitude toward compulsory arbitration. The severe condemnation of the system—judges, law, workers and all—reached its climax in 1917 when the Mount Morgan Miners' case was decided. In this case, the miners demanded union preference and Justice Macawley of the Arbitration Court granted their demand. The President of the Queensland Employers' Federation attacked the miners and the judge in harsh language saying that there were " unfortunate people " in Queensland who held the view that preference was justifiable, and that " similar cowardly expedients at the expense of conscience and principle have ever been rejected down the course of history." He went on to denounce the law, declaring that " laws and judges have withered before the breath of freedom." This spirit of hostility persisted throughout the troublesome years of the War and it continues to mold the opinion of the employers up to the present day.

This complete change of attitude towards arbitration demonstrates the essential difficulties of the system. It demonstrates two salient factors which govern the entire system of compulsory arbitration. These two vital elements are, namely, politics and human nature. When a new law concerning industrial matters is enacted, it registers the majority opinion of a legislature. But the majority frequently changes, and so the law is subject to constant alteration. A fuller discussion on these points, however, must be deferred for the next chapter. Suffice it to call attention to its importance at this juncture.

The policy of the Court up to 1920 was determined solely

by the Judges of the Court. But since the report of the Federal Basic Wage Commission in 1920, the Court, so far as the adjustment of wages is concerned, has been guided by the findings of that commission. The Court has come to realize more and more the economic principles involved in the fixing of wages. The influence of any fact-fiinding commission of this nature on the determinations of the Court should never be understimated. When the Court accepts the findings of the commission, the Court in reality becomes an administrative tribunal executing the orders of the commission.

The tendency to seek for authorities on economic questions for the purpose of shaping the policy of the Court became more marked when the Court created the Economic Commission in December, 1924. Justice Macawley, then Justice of the Court, when facing difficulties in determining a basic wage, created the commission to investigate the different factors influencing a basic wage and make recommendations as to the course to be pursued by the Court. The duty of the commission was to report on the six major considerations relating to the fixing of a basic wage. The major considerations were: (1) the prosperity of Queensland from 1913 to 1924; (2) the real wages compared with productivity for the same period; (3) the extent to which the adjustment of wages to variation in productivity is justifiable; (4) the effect of an increase of wages on the growth of industries in the State; (5) the probable consequences of an increase in the basic wage; and (6) other matters of economic nature which the commission may desire to offer.

1. The commission, after a two-months investigation, made its report in March, 1925.[1] It emphasized as its first recommendation that in declaring a basic wage for industries of average prosperity, the capacity of the industries

[1] *Queensland Industrial Gazette*, March, 1925, pp. 185-214.

to pay should be the chief consideration. The cost of living is to be considered only after the capacity to pay has been ascertained. This recommendation contradicts the policy of the Commonwealth Arbitration Court which declared that wages are independent of profit.

The commission was of the opinion that the productivity of Queensland, according to the value of products using 1911 as a base, has steadily increased, but the volume of primary production has decreased.[1]

2. As to the comparison of real wages and the capacity to produce, the commission found that from 1911 to 1916 the volume of production per head in the industries maintained a high level, but the value of production per head in the industries during the same period maintained a level comparatively lower than that of recent years. Real wages, on the other hand, remained for the whole decade below their 1911 base. The rise of real wages since 1921 has outstripped the yearly volume of production per head. Yet since 1922, the value of production per head increased over the advance of the rate of real wages.

3. With respect to the extent to which the adjustment of wages to variations in productivity, is justifiable, the commission asserted that the Court in fixing wages had not been practicing the principle of differentiating industries in a prosperous condition save in some very exceptional cases. The commission proposed that the Court should consider this matter with greater emphasis, for " it is not desirable that all workers should be paid the same rate for the same work done irrespective of the conditions of the industries." [2]

4. In regard to the question of the effect of the increase of wages upon an industry, the commission refrained from reaching any definite conclusion. It held, however, that in

[1] *Op. cit.*, pp. 197 and 200.

[2] *Ibid.*, p. 206.

general, "an increase in wages, so long as it can be paid by the representative firm, will tend to have the same effect. It will either force out the least efficient or compel them to become more efficient." By reciting this economic principle, the commission evaded the question of basic wage.

Should the recommendations of the commission be adopted, there will be an important change in policy since in the determination of wages the principle of cost of living will be made subordinate to the principle of capacity of the industry to pay. Another serious matter is the rejection of the doctrine of equal pay for equal work. While the attitude of the employers towards the report is naturally favorable, the workers by no means agree with these conclusions.

The forces which continue to operate in the system of compulsory arbitration will be further clarified by an analysis of the Commonwealth's experiment with this system.

V. COMPULSORY ARBITRATION IN THE AUSTRALIAN COMMONWEALTH

Inasmuch as the provisions of the Commonwealth Arbitration Law show no marked differences in principle from those of the New South Wales system, a brief description of it will serve the purpose of this essay. The Federal Constitution first came into operation on January 1, 1901, and there is a provision in this Federal Constitution which gives the Commonwealth the power to enact measures for the adjustment of labor disputes. Three years after the formation of the Federal Government, the Commonwealth Conciliation and Arbitration Act was enacted into law.

The Commonwealth Conciliation and Arbitration Act of 1904 was enacted on the model of the New South Wales' law of 1892. In many points these two laws are similar, as, for example, in the matter of the registration of industrial organizations or the cancellation of registrations. With regard to the powers of the Court or penalties imposed in the enforcement of its awards, the Commonwealth Arbitration law is a duplicate of that of New South Wales. The similarity holds true with respect to industrial agreements and the fixing of a minimum wage by the Court.

Nevertheless there are various points of difference. The distinguishing feature of the Commonwealth Act is its attempt to supplement the state laws. The Commonwealth Act deals with disputes arising outside the jurisdiction of any one state. An industrial dispute is defined as a dispute in relation to industrial matters "extending beyond the limits of any one state", including disputes in relation to employment upon state railways, and other employment in industries operated by the government, but it does not include a dispute relating to employment in any agricultural, viticultural, horticultural or dairying pursuit.

The "President" of the Court is appointed by the Governor General from the members of the High Court. He is entitled to hold office for seven years and is eligible for reappointment. Whenever the Court takes up a case, the state industrial courts cease their activities and leave the entire matter to the judgment of the Commonwealth body. In case the award of a state arbitration court is inconsistent with that of the Commonwealth Arbitration Court, the latter prevails, and the former is declared invalid. The Court has power to declare any common rule provided notification of the same has been published in the *Gazette*.

Amendments to the principal act have been enacted in 1909, 1910, 1911, 1914, 1915 and 1918. In the first amendment, in 1909, the significant clause inserted was the section extending or specifying the power of the President of the Court. The President of the Court may, subject to the approval of the Governor-General, makes rules not inconsistent with this act for regulating the practice and procedure of the Court.

By the amending act of 1910 four important changes were effected: (1) The definition of industry in the principal act was altered. The exception of agricultural pursuits, etc. was struck out. (2) The President of the Court was given power to summon any person at any time and place to attend a conference for the prevention or settlement of an industrial dispute. Disobedience of such a summons is punishable by a fine of five hundred pounds. (3) The power of the Court was further increased by a new provision. The principal act provided that in the matter of fixing minimum wages or granting preference to an organization, when a party had applied for either of these, the Court should make provision enabling some tribunal to fix the minimum wage or grant union preference. By the amending act, however, the Court is directed to settle such matters itself when proper application is made. (4) In order to increase the efficiency of the Court, "a board of reference" consisting of one or more persons may be created for the purpose of approving, fixing, or dealing with the awards.

The amendment of 1911 introduced two alterations. The principal act defined industry to mean "business, trade, manufacture, undertaking, calling, service, or employment, on land or water, in which persons are employed for pay, hire, advantage, or reward excepting only persons engaged in domestic service and persons engaged in agricultural, viticultural, horticultural, or dairying pursuits. . . ." The exceptions specified were struck out and industry defined to include: "(a) any business, trade, manufacture, undertaking, or calling of employers, on land or water; (b) any calling, service, employment, handicraft, or industrial occupation or avocation of employees, on land or water; and (c) a branch of an industry and a group of industries." [1]

[1] Section 4, Act 1904-1911.

Moreover, this amendment increased the penalty from twenty pounds to fifty pounds for offense by employers who dismiss any employee from their employment for the reason that this employee is entitled to the benfit of an award. And in case an employee ceases work solely because his employer receives the benefit of an award, he shall be fined twenty-five pounds instead of ten. The other amendments of 1914, 1915 and 1918 propose minor changes which do not affect the principle of the Act and may be eliminated from this discussion.

The result of the system has been admirably analyzed in a treatise entitled *A New Province for Law and Order* by H. B. Higgins, President of the Commonwealth Arbitration Court for nearly fourteen years. He succeeded the first president justice in 1907 but resigned in 1920 in protest over the passage of the Industrial Peace Act which, in his opinion, had transferred the power of the Court to some special tribunals.

The Industrial Peace Act of 1920 provides for the creation of special tribunals to deal with particular industrial disputes which the Court fails to adjust. A special tribunal of this nature consists of equal representatives of employers and employees, together with a chairman chosen by mutual agreement. In default of agreement, he shall be appointed by the Governor-General. The tribunal possesses all the powers which were conferred upon the Arbitration Court by the Commonwealth Conciliation and Arbitration Act of 1904-1918.

Justice Higgins protests that the new policy adopted encourages disputes, for a union when dissatisfied with the Court's award can bring the dispute to a special tribunal to deal with the matter anew—taking what is acceptable in the decision of the Court and insisting on a new award for the rest of its demands. " It is hard to conceive of a more effective device for encouraging industrial stoppages and for making the work of the Court ineffective."[1] Moreover, Justice Higgins raises another objection. "The Industrial Peace Act provides that the Court shall not make any award or order inconsistent with the award of the special tribunal; but there is no provision *e converso* that the special tribunal shall not make any award inconsistent with the award of the Court." In the light of these two serious objections to the Industrial Peace Act, it is plainly shown that the power of the Court has been greatly limited. It will be profitable, however, to examine the policies of the Court with respect to the different industrial issues.

The first question concerning wages is the minimum rates. A minimum wage, according to the practice of the Commonwealth Arbitration Court, is not the lowest rate payable to any employee, but the combination of a basic wage or primary wage and the secondary wage. By basic wage, or primary wage, is meant that rate which is assigned to unskilled laborers on the basis of "the normal needs of the average employee regarded as a human being living in a civilized community." The basic wage is then really the minimum standard wage for all normal unskilled labor. By secondary wage is meant the compensation for skill payable to the worker for the exercise of his exceptional abilities.

The fixing of a primary wage depends entirely on the cost of living. The same class of work then may be paid differently in the different parts of the country because of the variation of the cost of living among the different sections of the country. However, the basic wage or living wage fixed by the Court varies but very slightly from one district to another. The Court makes no independent investigation into the cost of living in Australia, but relies entirely upon the

[1] Higgins, H. B., *A New Province for Law and Order*, 1922, p. 164.

Commonwealth Statisticians' report. The cost of living for 1907 which was computed to be 42s per week met little opposition at the time. But as the years go by, there have been strenuous attacks on the Commonwealth Statistician's figures. The employers' reason for their vigorous attacks on the scheme is that while they yield to the order of the Court to grant wages in the event of a rise in the cost of living, the Court does not always reduce wages when circumstances demand. On the other hand, the workers argue that wages always lag behind the cost of living. As soon as their wages increase, they find that the prices of food, clothing and shelter augment at greater rates.[1]

In connection with the matter of basic wage, it is interesting to observe the findings of the Basic Wage Commission of 1920. The Commission held that a basic wage is not the necessary subsistence wage for an unskilled laborer, but a living wage computed "according to reasonable standards of comfort, including all matter comprised in the ordinary expenditure of a household, for a man and his wife and three children under fourteen years of age." The Commission proposes a cost of living far in excess of the basic wage fixed by the Court at the time. The Commission found that the basic wage for Melbourne should be £5 16s 6d per week, but it did not recommend the enforcement of this standard. The unions combined to press for the adoption of the new rate, but the Court refused to grant the liberal standard set up by the Commission. The bone of contention seemed to be the interpretation of the term "reasonable standards of comfort." For what is reasonable for one class of workers may not be reasonable for another. It is apparent that the principle needs some more definite elucidation.

Another element in the problem of wages is the deter-

[1] Australian Commonwealth, *Labor Report No. 7*, 1917.

mination of the secondary wage. By secondary wage is meant, as it has just been defined, the compensation for the additional or exceptional gifts or qualifications necessary for the performance of the work required. This includes the several considerations of skill, training and responsibility. The necessity for the secondary wage lies in the maintenance of skilled labor, for there must be sufficient inducement for the cultivation of extra skill in order that the supply of skilled labor be continued. The fixing of minimum rates for skilled labor is no easy matter.

A necessary corollary to the principles of primary and secondary wages is a special rate for aged and slow workers, which may be termed a "defective" or "abnormal wage." It is obvious that if a minimum wage is imposed upon an employer, he will select only young men who will bring him the maximum return. The aged and infirm workers would be entirely displaced by more efficient workers, and the distress of unemployment would prove a burden to the community. The Court was compelled by economic principles to fix a lower rate for slow workers. In fact, this matter of a lower rate for slow workers is an important provision of the Act as well as a fundamental mandate of the economic law of wages.

The most progressive step pursued by the Court concerning the adjustment of wages is the policy of fixing wages independent of profit. This policy has been maintained since its first introduction in the Broken Hill Mine case of 1909.[1] In this case, as well as in subsequent decisions, the Court held that the fact that a mine was becoming exhausted was not a ground for prescribing a lower rate of wages than the Law permitted. Wages form a part of the cost of an

[1] Broken Hill Mine, *Commonwealth Arbitration Report*, vol. iii, p. 1 (1909); Shearers, 5 *C. A. R.* 48 (1911); Ship Officers, 6 *C. A. R.* 6 (1912); Engine-Drivers 7, *C. A. R.* 132 (1913).

industry and ought to be charged on the industry as a necessary cost of its operation. "The Court cannot endanger industrial peace in order to keep unprofitable mines going." The adherence of the Court to this policy manifests a clear vision of the noble principle that a country is not its mines, nor its money, but its men.

In regard to the matter of hours of work, the Court fixes no absolute standard of hours for all classes. It follows the principle of variation of hours according to the nature of the work. Before 1920, however, the Court had generally conceded to some industries the forty-eight-hour week to be divided into 8¾ hours for five days and 4¼ hours for Saturday. The eight-hour day, strictly speaking, did not generally exist. But since the Australian Timber Workers' case of 1920,[1] the eight-hour day has been definitely and generally established. In this case the Court conceded the forty-eight-hour week. The significance of this case lies in the fact that there are many industries of similar character, and when the Court decided to grant the forty-eight-hour week to the timber workers, it had to make similar decisions for all other employees hitherto regarded as doing a similar class of work.

However, it should be observed that there are exceptions to this general rule. The Court justifies a reduction of hours from the general rule chiefly upon two grounds, namely, the exceptional strain of work upon the workers' mind[2] and the loss of time in carrying on work at a different location.[3] On the other hand, there are occupations in which the fifty-two-hour week still prevails. Certain classes of carters and drivers are cases in point.[4]

[1] 14 *C. A. R.* 811 (1920)

[2] Gas Employees, 11 *C. A. R.* (1917).

[3] Broken Hill 10 *C. A. R.* 155 (1916).

[4] Butchers 10 *C. A. R.* 496 (1916).

It is only fair to say that so far as wages and hours are concerned compulsory arbitration has benefited the workers in Australia. It has destroyed sweating and it has also raised the wages of unskilled labor to a higher level. True, the various investigations have shown that the increase in the rate of wages has lagged behind the increase in the cost of living. But considering other circumstances, the Court seems to have done the best that was practicable. Besides the questions of wages and hours, there are two more significant points which require a brief treatment. They are, namely, the question of union preference and the degree of success in the prevention of strikes.

As to the first point, the Court has never but once in its entire history granted union preference. It possesses full power to grant or to refuse preference; it has chosen the latter policy. The Court is slow in the exercise of the power of granting union preference because it maintains the theory that an employer should have an absolute power of choosing his employees so that the most capable men available may be secured.[1] It regards union preference as a defense against union discrimination rather than as a method of promoting unionism or a reward to the unionists for their obedience of and loyalty to the Act. "The truth is, preference is sought for unionists in order to prevent preference of non-unionists or anti-unionists—to prevent the gradual bleeding of unionism by the feeding of non-unionism. It is a weapon of defense."[2] In pursuance of this policy, the Court granted union preference to the tramway workers in 1912 because the tramway company deliberately discriminated against unionists and refused to alter its policy in the future.[3]

[1] Marine Engineers, 6 *C. A. R.* 95 (1912); Engine-drivers 5 *C. A. R.* 9 (1911); Shearers 5 *C. A. R.* 48 (1911); Seamen 5 *C. A. R.* 147 (1911); Builders' laborers 7 *C. A. R.* 210 (1913).

[2] Builders' laborers 7 *C. A. R.* 210 (1913) at p. 233.

[3] Tramways, 6 *C. A. R.* 130 (1912).

With respect to the prevention of strikes, the Court has done no better and no worse than the criminal courts in their efforts to eliminate crimes. Notwithstanding that from 1904 to 1915 there had been no strikes of a national character, the absence of strikes of this nature might not have been due to the good service of the Court. Justice Higgins claimed that much ground had been gained since the nineties at which time there occurred the shearers' strike and the seamen's strike, and that the prevention of nation-wide strikes was attributable to the Court. But there is ample reason for discounting this statement. During the nineties, there were no state agencies for adjusting labor disputes and whenever strikes occurred, they had a tendency to spread throughout the principal sections of the country. But since the inauguration of the state agencies, the different states have undertaken to settle disputes which arose within their borders. Moreover, not long after Justice Higgins formally set forth the result of the Law for the first time,[1] serious strikes within the jurisdiction of the Court broke out. They occurred first in October, 1916, in the miners' case, then there was the glass bottle makers' strike in June, 1917, and the engineers' strike in August of the same year. The strikes of a national character increase as the years go by. The seamen struck in May, 1919, followed by the Marine Engineers' strike and then by the building trade employees and the gas workers in 1920, and finally the marine stewards in 1921. All these cases warrant the conclusion, not that compulsory arbitration has succeeded in preventing strikes, but that it has sadly failed. We have seen that it has failed in New Zealand and New South Wales. It has also been unsuccessful in the Commonwealth of Australia.

[1] In an article entitled, "A New Province of Law and Order," *Harvard Law Review*, Nov., 1915.

Finally, the most serious blow to the system, delivered after it had been in operation for more than a decade, was a decision of the Higher Court in the " Waterside Workers *v.* Alexander " case.[1] In this case the Higher Court declared that the purport of the Arbitration Act invested the Arbitration Court with power to enforce its decision, according to section 71 and 72 of the constitution, but no judge can exercise that power unless he has a life tenure. The President of the Arbitration Court has not a life tenure, and the court, therefore, cannot exercise that power. The heart of the compulsory arbitration law in the Commonwealth seems to have been entirely taken out.

[1] 25 *C. L. R.* 434 (1918).

CHAPTER VII

Conclusion

I. RECAPITULATION

This thesis begins with definitions of terms and a classification of the existing governmental methods of adjusting labor disputes in North America and Australasia. The basis for the classification of the different methods is the degree of power exercised by the government.

Next, the essay proceeds to deal with the system of adjusting labor disputes in the different states of the United States. The discussion starts with tentative mediation in Georgia, and continues with positive mediation in Pennsylvania, New York, and Ohio. Furthermore, it analyzes voluntary arbitration in Massachusetts, compulsory investigation in Colorado, obligatory arbitration in South Carolina, and quasi-judicial adjudication in Kansas. It has been observed that compulsory arbitration is contrary to the Constitution of the United States, and that for this reason, the Kansas Act of Industrial Relations has been declared unconstitutional.

Chapter III analyzes the policies of the United States towards railroad labor disputes. The entire history of Federal intervention in railroad labor controversies is divided into three distinct periods. The first period extended from 1888, when the first arbitration act dealing with railroad labor differences was passed, to the outbreak of the World War. During this period positive mediation and voluntary arbitration prevailed. The second period included all the years of the War, from its outbreak to its termination. During this second period, the Adamson Law was passed and wage-board adjustment was put into operation. The significance of the Adamson Law lies not so much in its provisions as in the demonstration of a new policy of the Government which it signalizes in enforcing agreement between employers and employees by means of legislative enactment. The Supreme Court of the United States in upholding this law proposed a new argument for labor legislation. It declared that the "unusual circumstances" warranted the action of Congress. The last period commenced with the passage of the Transportation Act of 1920 which provides for advisory determination. The prolongation of this policy depends upon the continuation of the Republican administration as well as the efficient administration of the Labor Board and the tolerance of the men and management.

Chapter IV describes the Canadian Industrial Investigation Act, its provisions and its results. It has been emphasized that compulsory investigation, when properly conducted proves advantageous to all parties concerned, employers and employees as well as the public. The suggestion is made that an amendment of the section concerning the prohibition of strikes and lockouts is desirable. The reason for this proposal is that a strike, in order to be effective must be declared at a strategic time, but the law, by prohibiting the strike before or during investigation, renders the weapon for collective bargaining ineffective. True, at the same time the lockout is made unlawful, but the latter requires no strategic time to accomplish its end.

Finally, chapters V and VI deal with the methods of adjusting labor disputes in Australasia. The center of interest in these chapters is the system of compulsory arbitration. It has been pointed out that New Zealand was the first country which inaugurated compulsory arbitration but that the system originated not in New Zealand but in South

Australia. With the exceptions of Victoria and Tasmania, which are experimenting with wage-board adjustment, all the Australian states as well as the Commonwealth of Australia have adopted the machinery of compulsory arbitration. A study of the experiments shows that compulsory arbitration, as it operates in New Zealand and Australia, has benefited the laboring classes. Among the various progressive measures, the granting of union preference works decidedly to the advantage of labor. Furthermore, the policy pursued by the Australian Commonwealth Arbitration Court in fixing wages independent of profits illustrates another advantage to labor. The greatest objection to the system, however, lies in its failure to enforce the provisions of the law. The attempt to prevent strikes and lockouts by compulsory arbitration has proven a complete failure, for no artificial means of this nature can ever be successful in destroying the human desire for self-government.

Thus, the foregoing chapters have exhausted the subject in all its fundamental aspects. This remaining chapter will summarize the general principles and problems involved in the three important methods of adjusting labor disputes, namely, voluntary arbitration, compulsory investigation and compulsory arbitration.

II. THE PRINCIPLES AND PROBLEMS OF VOLUNTARY ARBITRATION

The principles of voluntary arbitration are based on the theory that when disputants cannot settle their disagreement themselves, a third party may often step in and adjust the difference. Voluntary arbitration rests on the spirit of concession as the foundation upon which the whole edifice is built. In case either of the disputants refuses to submit its case to the judgment of an outsider, voluntary arbitration fails. It fails because the spirit of compromise is wanting. But if the disputants are ready to reach a compromise, and both try to avoid warfare, voluntary arbitration certainly will prove an effective measure. The term itself, in fact, signifies that success depends entirely upon the attitude of the opposing parties.

The advantages of voluntary arbitration may be considered from two standpoints: the beneficial aspect of arbitration proceedings and the humanitarian effect of arbitration. The actual proceedings in connection with arbitration cases are recorded by all responsible boards. These records are of great help in the adjustment of similar cases without tests of strength on every issue. The interpretation of precedents in itself makes for a gain in efficiency. Moreover, the boards study the precedents and from these they draw conclusions. Cases settled by arbitration may form the foundation for later legislation, just as judicial precedents may establish a common rule. Furthermore, the immense economy of arbitration may readily be seen when the losses resulting from industrial war are estimated. Arbitral awards are by no means easy to foresee, but it is still more difficult to compute the probable outcome of an industrial battle. Disputants will choose arbitration in preference to strikes and lockouts unless they have reached the conclusion that a combat may bring greater spoil than a compromise.

One of the inevitable consequences of arbitration is the recognition of equality between the parties. For this reason labor unions, except highly organized unions which have been disappointed by previous arbitral decisions, are often the ones to initiate arbitration as a means for the adjustment of differences. When employers consent to arbitrate differences with their employees, the respective positions are no longer of masters and servants, but of men and men.

The difficulties of arbitration, however, are many and

complicated. They fall chiefly under three heads: (1) the question of the impartiality of the arbitrators, (2) the efficiency of the methods of procedure, and (3) the basis for the awards.

The difficulty of securing the right men for arbitrators really constitutes the chief objection to arbitration. In the first place, competent men are not always available. The division of labor in industries has proved a complicated process, and without technical knowledge of the industry it is difficult to judge the merits of any controversial issue. Moreover, provided that men of technical ability are available, the question of their impartiality as arbitrators still remains. Basil M. Manly, a former joint chairman of the United States National War Labor Board, although perhaps too one-sided in his criticism of the alleged partiality of the arbitrator, has clearly analyzed the problem.[1] He points out that "where personal and class interests are so largely involved in the determination of an issue as in the settlement of industrial disputes, it is almost inevitable that every member of an arbitration board should be biased in one direction or the other."[2] He points out further that the arbitrators are necessarily biased because they are drawn generally from the professional classes, that is, judges, lawyers, teachers and preachers. The fact that their occupations have no direct interest in a particular industry cannot be a guarantee of their impartiality. Forces exist which indirectly influence their judgment. Mr. Manly amplifies his idea by tracing a few of these forces which are at work in arbitration proceedings. His conclusions are valuable. He says:

[1] Manly, Basil M., "Arbitration and Industrial Justice," *Survey*, April 8, 1922, p. 44.

[2] *Ibid.*, *Survey*, April 8, 1922, p. 45.

The *class consciousness*[1] on the part of all but a few exceptional individuals inevitably influences their judgment. Their daily associations are confined almost entirely to the employing class. They hear daily in clubs, drawingrooms, offices and Pullman cars one-sided stories of the troubles which the employer has over labor inefficiency, union domination, restriction of output, and all the other difficulties experienced in his industrials [industry] but they seldom hear at first hand of troubles of the workers. The reading of the professional classes is confined almost entirely to the daily press and other publications which, to say the least, are not edited with the object of presenting the workers' point of view in the most favorable light. . . .

Equally important is the fact that the *personal interests*[1] of an overwhelming proportion of the professional classes are directly or indirectly dependent upon the interests of the employers. Most professional men have investments in industrial enterprises. These investments may be only a few hundred or a few thousand dollars, but they tend to influence the judgment of those who hold them.

Finally, there is that fact that the *income*[1] [incomes] of the great majority of professional men are dependent upon the favor of employers, and that only a small percentage are in any way affected by the disfavor of trade unions or individual workers. . . . Nine-tenths of the lawyers are dependent upon corporation practice. Less directly, but none the less inevitably, are the other professions dependent upon the favor of employers and corporations.

Assuming that the difficulty concerning the partiality of the supposed neutral arbitrators has been overcome, industrial arbitration still cannot free itself altogether from the obstacles which hinder its progress in the promotion of industrial harmony. The second special difficulty has reference to the procedure of arbitration. The representatives

[1] Italics mine.

of each side necessarily maintain a partisan attitude. Each of them fights for the party which he represents. Lengthy discussion may prove a great disadvantage to labor because with delay the strike as a weapon may lose its effectiveness.

Moreover, employers usually find themselves in a better position during arbitration proceedings than their employees, for the obvious reason that the former possesses all necessary documents, books and records from which they may draw arguments in their favor. So long as they keep secret the figures relative to profits, there can be no adequate way of determining a satisfactory arbitration award. Employers who desire to maintain high profits are likely to declare that any increase in wages will cut profit to the bone, curtail investment, and destroy industry. The inability to pay always constitutes the chief argument against wage increases. Equally strong assertions are presented by the employees. Profit, they argue, is excessive. Wages are too low. Thus Samuel Gompers has rightly declared that " To say that an industry does not admit, or will not allow, the payment of a living wage is a libel upon the human race." [1] " Low wages have vicious effects upon national vigor and power—poorly paid workers usually deteriorate in physical and mental ability and in power to produce." [2] The arbitrators in consequence of these conflicting opinions are entirely at sea.

III. THE PRINCIPLES AND PROBLEMS OF COMPULSORY INVESTIGATION

Compulsory investigation, like voluntary arbitration, rests also on the possibility of mutual understanding. The purpose of investigation is partly to facilitate a better understanding of the positions between the contestants by specific

[1] Samuel Gompers, *Labor and the Employer*, New York, 1920, p. 62.

[2] *Ibid.*, p. 105.

findings. It has been a matter of common occurrence that in disputes between labor and capital, both parties have sincerely and honestly believed themselves to be fighting for justice. Each party is blind to the limitations of and the reasons for the other side. Machinery for investigation in such cases clearly demonstrates its usefulness.

The last resort for the enforcement of an award of compulsory investigation must necessarily be the force of public opinion. The system presupposes, therefore, that public opinion is keen to condemn the side which brings the inconvenience upon the public. Undoubtedly, the public is always alert when its interest is subject to an actual menace. This third party, however, usually remains in silence partly due to its indifference to the dispute and partly to its ignorance of the many questions involved. The cure for its indifference is not difficult to suggest. Any peaceful community may be aroused to war hysteria by a call to arms because of some alleged injustice or impending danger. Many a fighting mob too may be won over by an eloquent appeal to its emotions and impulses. By such means as this, Mark Antony swayed the crowd at the Roman Forum, which mourned over Caesar's tragic death and made them all cry for revenge on the assassins: "Revenge! About! Seek! Burn! Fire! Kill! Slay! Let not a traitor live!" On the other hand, the battle with ignorance is a hard struggle. The purpose of investigation is, therefore, chiefly educational.

Compulsory investigation encounters three serious barriers: first, the difficulty of bringing the parties to an agreement to submit their differences to official investigation; second, the difficulty of securing accurate information of the real situation; and third, the problem of prosecution or enforcement.

1. In spite of the compulsory provision of a compulsory

investigation law, it is not an uncommon occurrence, as in Canada, that disputants resort to the illegal practices of strikes and lockouts rather than to the legal practices of government investigation. When the fighting spirit of any party runs high, a fight to a finish must eventually be the consequence. The refusal of a disputant to submit its case to government investigation, however, has not always been on sentimental grounds. The workingmen are not unreasable in their argument that their fundamental right to strike is the only effective weapon by which they may expect redress for their grievances, and that compulsory investigation abrogates this right. The provision for compulsory investigation requires that no strike or lockout should occur before or during investigation, and this provision gives the employers the advantage of having sufficient time to make preparation to meet the emergency, in case it should occur.

2. The difficulty of securing accurate information is due in part to technical obstacles and in part to scarcity of available material. Given the same data, different statistical methods produce different results. A different attitude in approaching a problem often leads to divergent conclusions. On the other hand, the scarcity of reliable data available greatly hampers an impartial investigation.

3. Finally, the ultimate question of enforcement has presented the greatest difficulties to all laws of this nature. A compulsory investigation law provides that breach of agreement or award is punishable by a fine not exceeding a certain amount of money or imprisonment not exceeding a certain number of months. The question is: Could the Government prosecute any violation of this restrictive clause? So far as the Canadian experiment is concerned, numerous offenses have led to but few prosecutions. It is impossible to put a thousand or more men in prison at the same time, and it is equally impracticable to levy fines on

strikers in such numbers when they refuse to pay. The collection of the fines creates a huge task which requires the maintenance of a large force of government officials. Politically, as well as economically, it is an unwise measure to repress strikes when conditions become unbearable; for so long as inhuman working conditions exist, no human hand can by any magic wave create thunderbolts terrible and merciless enough to destroy the rebellious desire of men. Until the causes of strikes are removed, the souls of the toiling millions will not be at rest.

IV. THE PRINCIPLES AND PROBLEMS OF COMPULSORY ARBITRATION

Compulsory arbitration finds its justification in the safeguarding of the public interest. Under the system of compulsory arbitration, strikes and lockouts are made crimes against the public on the ground that they impose inconveniences upon the public. The theory is, moreover, that civilization exacts, as the price for greater comfort, a stricter observance of law and order. A community can no more tolerate the crippling of production and the interruption of supplies of necessities essential to its life and safety than injuries done to individual properties. Therefore, when strikes occur, the government assumes the position of an impartial arbitrator and enforces a judgment, substituting legal proceedings for industrial wars.

Compulsory arbitration, so far as the question of human nature is concerned, encounters all the difficulties which confront voluntary arbitration. The operation of compulsory arbitration, moreover, creates specific problems distinctly its own. Some of the chief problems of the system are, namely: (1) the question of wages, (2) hours, (3) union preference, (4) the selection of judges, (5) partisan representation, (6) the enforcement of awards and (7) the coordination of the inter-judicial relations between Federal and State courts.

1. The inauguration of a minimum wage appears to have been an inevitable result of compulsory arbitration. Even in countries where compulsory arbitration has not won legal acceptance, minimum wage legislation has been adopted. In every Australian state, the idea of the basic wage has become a part of its arbitration law. The regulation of wages brings about a train of relevant problems. The determination of the cost of living and the ability of the industry to pay seem to have been the outstanding obstacles confronting the Australian arbitration courts. Besides these difficulties, the court has had to determine arbitrarily secondary wages which are fixed in accordance with the relative skill of the employees and the nature of the employment. The immensity of the task of fixing and revising the wage schedules can easily be imagined.

2. The question of fixing the number of working hours is comparatively simpler than the adjustment of the scale of wages, but it is no less arbitrary. The difficulty of determining a reduction of hours lies mainly in the ascertainment of the practicability of reducing the number of hours for similar classes of work in accordance with the standard set up for a class. If an arbitration court grants a forty-four hour week to one class of workers, it should be prepared to grant the same to all other classes who are doing work of similar nature. The nature of the work, therefore, has been the chief criterion for the determination of the working hours. The hours for deep-shaft mining will necessarily differ from those for pastoral pursuits. Between these two extremes, however, there are classes of work in which physical exhaustion as well as mental strain show small variations and can never be accurately measured. The granting of a reduction of hours to one class will necessitate

a general rule applicable to all similar classes. In a roundabout way, the ability of related industries to stand the reduction of hours enters again into the complicated calculation.

3. Union preference is another inevitable issue in connection with compulsory arbitration, for the system definitely recognizes collective bargaining. A compulsory arbitration law will defeat its own object, if it discourages unionism. A large part of the unconquered territory would remain beyond the control of its legal machinery, were it not for the existence and proper functioning of the union.

The justifications for union preference center in five main points: first, the encouragement to unions for the sake of maintaining professional standards of skill and honor; second, the principle of judgment by result; third, the principle of neutrality; fourth, the principle of majority rule; and fifth, the reward of the union which complies with the law in good faith in the promotion of industrial peace. Unionism, in the mind of the organized workers, is almost a religion. It stands for an ideal—the ideal of concerted action for the protection of individual and social welfare. For this reason, it has a right to demand that every worker who performs a certain duty should conform to the standard set up by the union, and that the best guarantee for a satisfactory standard can only be secured through the employment of union men. The last justification for preference, that if a union abides by the awards of the court and has kept its allegiance to the law in good faith, preference should be given unionists as a reward for their obedience and loyalty, appears to be a desirable policy for the sake of making compulsory arbitration more effective.

The objections to union preference, however, fortify themselves on the strong ground of personal liberty. By giving preference to unionists, the employers abrogate their rights in the choice of their employees. Even from the workers' point of view, union preference tends to interfere with the workers' individual liberty. It gives the opportunity for union leaders to control their members in seeking employment. Unless the unions are well regulated, the control of a large majority of workers by a few union officials would be a transformation of democracy into autocracy. Moreover, under the system of party politics, an industrial union is inevitably drawn into political contests. The danger of union preference is that it intimidates the individual with the penalty of losing his union membership if he insists on his independent opinon on certan political issues. He is liable to be a slave to mob psychology. The union bosses may become party bosses, and few would dare to challenge their orders, for few are prepared to drink the hemlock of the martyr. However, these defects are not incurable. Safeguards against unjust practices may be incorporated in the law which grants union preference. The law may prescribe that no organization shall be entitled to preference unless it refrains from permitting application of its funds for political purposes, and abstains from requiring its members to fulfill any duty that is of a political character, and that the conditions of admission and discharge from the union must be fair and reasonable.

4. As the selection of arbitrators is a vital problem in voluntary arbitration, an even more serious problem is the selection of the judges of a compulsory arbitration court. The judges may alter the scale of wages to such an extent as to entirely wipe out profits, or to such a degree as to cut wages to the bone. They may grant preference to all unions and they may make common rules of many practices and regulations. When the welfare of the community depends on the judgment of one or two individuals the importance of their selection can scarcely be exaggerated. Impartial individuals who honestly believe their opinions to be just

and fair, are not difficult to find. But the problem lies in the point of view they hold with respect to certain economic and legal questions. Practically every controversy creates a new circumstance and demands a new attitude, a new outlook. In every judgment, the judges are likely to be subject to the influences of their previous training, their associations and more or less their personal interests.

5. Closely related to the problem of the selection of judges is the question of partisan representation. In all voluntary arbitration proceedings, partisan members are always present to defend their respective sides. But the question has risen as to the advisability of partisan representation in a compulsory arbitration tribunal. It is the practice in New Zealand to appoint partisan representatives. According to the Kansas plan, however, industrial disputes should be subject to the judgment of a judicial body just as any civil or criminal case is adjudicated by a judicial tribunal.

The chief objections against partisan representation are: first, the tendency to lengthen the arbitration proceedings causing unnecessary delay, and second, the danger of exposing the public interest to party quarrels. The first objection has been borne out by facts. In all controversies, each side tries to present its case to the fullest extent. The testimony of witnesses often consumes a large portion of the time. The second objection, however, remains a controversial matter. The argument that partisan representation would result in a conspiracy or agreement deterimental to the public interest, is invalid. Undoubtedly, an increase of prices often follows an increase of wages and the burden often falls upon the consumers—the public at large. But this is no sound reason against partisan representation. The increase in prices, caused by the increase of wages, may happen in countries where the industrial courts are composed of so-called public representatives only. Wherever and whenever wages are arbitrarily raised, other things being equal, the increased cost of production has to be met by the raising of prices, unless the rate of profit has been so high that it can suffer a reduction without an increase of the market price of the commodity.

The arguments for partisan representation appear to be more convincing. A tribunal may go astray for lack of expert assistance, and partisan representation helps to supply this requirement for accurate knowledge. Arbitrators often are strangers to the very industry on which they are called to pass an intelligent judgment. It is not uncommon for learned judges to fail to understand the meaning of technical terms used in the industries they are examining. The advantage of getting the assistance of practical men from the field is only too obvious. Furthermore, the bringing of both parties to a conference will give to each a better understanding of the position of the opposing side. True, when both parties are in belligerent mood, hostility may be intensified by confronting them with opposing arguments. But when one side begins to see, even to a small extent, the point of view of the other side, the spirit of mutual understanding will foster a conciliatory attitude in which adjustments may be reached.

6. Provisions for the enforcement of arbitral decisions have nowhere been strictly observed. New South Wales has adopted the most progressive step in the prosecution of violation of awards by imposing fines on the strikers as a first charge against their wages. Nevertheless, this punishment fails to prevent strikes. The method of enforcement by imprisonment has been actually proved impracticable. The law may inflict penalties upon responsible labor leaders but clearly it is a physical impossibility to put a large body of men in jail at one time.

The greatest weakness of compulsory arbitration, therefore, is its failure to fulfill the purpose which it professes to achieve.

7. Finally, there is the problem of interjurisdictional overlapping between state and Federal laws. As forest fires which swept through artificial state lines require for their extinction the cooperation in united effort of neighboring states, and as railroads which necessarily run across state boundaries need Federal regulations, so the system of arbitration demands the cooperation of state and Federal authorities. The Australian shearers' case is an interesting example of this difficulty. The shearers in that country in the course of their employment move from one state to another, from one pastoral station to another, as the season advances. But different states pursue different policies with respect to the hours of work. The shearers when they were in Queensland, worked forty-four hours per week. But when they passed the boundary lines to New South Wales or South Australia, they were required to work forty-eight hours. And vice versa when the shearers of New South Wales cross the state line, they claim the legal maximum hours according to Queensland practice. This confusion constitutes an additional cause of dispute. The solution of this difficulty, however, will not be as easy as it seems, because in the smoothing out of the inconsistencies, local rights are involved.

All these problems and many others are bound to be encountered upon the introduction of compulsory arbitration. The advisability of adopting the system depends upon many factors. The chief elements are the character of the industry and the size of the working population. Where industrial development has reached a highly complex stage, and where the working population is large, compulsory arbitration is impracticable. The question of efficiency in administration weighs heavily against its adoption.

BIBLIOGRAPHY

Chapter II

Allen, H. J., *The Party of the Third Part*, Harpers, 1921.

Bowers, J. H., *Kansas Court of Industrial Relations*, McClurg, 1922.

California, *State Board of Arbitration Reports*, 1892-1894.

Colorado Compiled Laws, 1921, chap. lxxix.

Colorado Industrial Commission Annual Reports, 1916-1923.

Feis, Herbert, "The Kansas Court of Industrial Relations: Its Spokesmen, Its Record," *Quarterly Journal of Economics*, vol. xxxii, no. 4, August 1923.

——, "The Kansas Court and the National Strikes," *Survey*, December 15, 1922.

——, "Kansas Miners and the Kansas Court," *Survey*, February 25, 1922.

——, "Kansas Clings to Its Court," *Survey*, May 15, 1923.

——, *Principles of Wage Settlement*, H. W. Wilson, 1924.

Georgia, *Commission of Commerce and Labor Annual Reports*, 1911-1924.

Hatch, Leonard W., *Government Industrial Arbitration*, U. S. Bureau of Labor Statistics Bulletin No. 60.

Huggins, W. L., *Labour and Democracy*, Macmillan, 1922.

Illinois, *Arbitration Report*, 1896-1916.

Kansas Court of Industrial Relations: *Report*, 1920-1922.

Massachusetts, *Annual Report of the State Board of Conciliation and Arbitration*, 1887-1919.

Massachusetts Department of Labor and Industries Annual Report, 1920-1924.

Massachusetts General Law, 1921.

New York Department of Labor Annual Reports, 1900-1924.

New York Industrial Commission Bulletin, 1915-1922.

New York, *Report of the Bureau of Mediation and Arbitration*, 1887-1900.

Ohio Arbitration Board Reports, 1895-1905.

Pennsylvania Department of Labour and Industry Bulletin, 1920-1922.

South Carolina Statutes, Act No. 589, 1922.

U. S. Bureau of Labour Statistics, *Kansas Court of Industrial Relations*, Bulletin No. 322, April, 1923.

Wolff Packing Company Case: 109 *Kansas* 646 (1921).

United States Supreme Court: 262 *U. S.* 522 (1922); 299 *U. S.* (1924).

Chapter III

The American Federationist, 1897-1925.

Arbitration between the Brotherhood of Locomotive Firemen and Enginemen and the Eastern Railroads, 1913.

Award of Arbitration between Western Railroads and the Brotherhood of Locomotive Engineers and the Brotherhood of Locomotive Firemen and Enginemen, 1915.

Bing, Alexander M., *War-Time Strikes and Their Adjustment*, New York, 1921.

Bureau of Industrial Research, *How the Government Handled Its Labor Problems During the War.*

Conference on Wage Adjustment between the Eastern Railroads and the Brotherhood of Locomotive Engineers, 1912.

Congressional Record.

Fisher, C. O., *Use of Federal Power in Settlement of Railway Labour Disputes*, Bureau of Labour Statistics, Conciliation and Arbitration Series, *Bulletin* No. 303, 1922.

Industrial Conference Report (second), 1920.

McCabe, David A., Federal Intervention in Labour Disputes under the Erdman, Newlands and Adamson Acts, *Academy of Political Science Proceedings*, 1917, pp. 94-107.

Pennsylvania Railroad *vs.* U. S. Railroad Labor Board, 261 *U. S.* 72 (1922).

The Railway Conductor.

The Railroad Gazette, 1898-1925.

The Railway Telegrapher.

The Railway Worker.

Shea, Timothy, Pending Railroad Legislation, *Academy of Political Science Proceedings*, January, 1920, pp. 156-164.

United States Board of Mediation and Conciliation Report, 1913-1919.

United States Bureau of Labor Statistics, *Bulletin* No. 98.

United States Industrial Conference Report, Washington, 1920.

United States Congress, Committee of Interstate and Foreign Commerce, *Hearings on H. R. 22012 to amend the Erdman Act*, 1912.

——, *Hearings on S. 2646*, 1924.

United States Railroad Labor Board Decisions, vols. i, ii, iii and iv.

United States Railroad Labor Board, *Wage Series Report* No. 1.

United States Statutes, vol. xxv, chap. 1063; vol. xxx, chap. 370; vol xxxviii, chap. 370; vol. xxxix, chap. 436; vol. xli, chap. 91.

United States Supreme Court, 243 *U. S.* 332 (1916).

Chapter IV

Askwith (Lord), *Industrial Problems and Disputes*, 1912.

Canada, *Department of Labor Report*, 1908.

Canada, *Statutes*, 1901, 1906, 1907, 1910, 1918, 1920.

Canada Department of Labor, *Labour Gazette*, 1907-1925.

Clark, Victor S., The Canadian Industrial Disputes Act, *Academy of Political Science Proceedings*, vol. vii, pp. 10-18, January, 1917.

Edgar, William Wilkie, The Settlement of Industrial Disputes in Canada, *Journal of Political Economy*, vol. xvi, February, 1908, pp. 88-93.

National Industrial Conference Board, *Research Report* No. 5, April, 1918, revised and reprinted, April, 1920.

Selekman, Ben M., Nine Years of the Canadian Act, *Survey*, vol. 37, pp. 746-754, March 31, 1917.

Squires, Benjamin M., *The Industrial Disputes Investigation Act of Canada*, U. S. Bureau of Labour Statistics, *Bulletin* No. 233, July, 1918.

Survey, The Canadian Disputes Act a Symposium, vol. 37, pp. 754-759, March 31, 1917.

Chapter V

Hammond, M. B., Compulsory Arbitration in Australia and New Zealand, *Proceedings of the Academy of Political Science*, vol. vii, 1917-1918, pp. 19-30.

Le Rossignal, J. E., Compulsory Arbitration in New Zealand, *Quarterly Journal of Economics*, vol. xxiv, 1910, pp. 60-712.

National Industrial Conference Board (New York), *Conciliation and Arbitration in New Zealand, Research Report*, no. 23, December, 1919.

New Zealand Department of Labour, *Annual Reports of Awards, Agreements, Recommendations, etc.*, 1896-1924.

New Zealand Employers' Federation, *Industrial Bulletin*, 1914-1925.

New Zealand Statutes, 1894, 1895, 1896, 1898, 1900, 1901, 1903, 1906, 1908. nos. 82 and 239; 1911, no. 33.

Reeves, William Pember, *State Experiments in Australia and New Zealand*, 1902; revised, 1925.

Victorian Employers' Federation, *Compulsory Conciliation and Arbitration, Case against Them*, 1901.

Chapter VI

Australia, *Commonwealth Arbitration Reports*, 1905-1924.

Australian Commonwealth Bureau of Census, *Labour Branch Reports*, nos. 1-14, 1911-1923.

Australia, *Commonwealth Law Reports*.

Australian Commonwealth Statistician, *Australia Statistics Quarterly Summary*, 1914-1925.

Australian Workers' Union Official Report of Annual Convention, 1914-1923.

Higgins, H. B., *A New Province for Law and Order*, 1922.

National Industrial Conference Board (New York): *Arbitration and Wage Fixing in Australia, Research Report No. 10*, 1918.

New South Wales Arbitration Court Reports, 1902-1925.

New South Wales Board of Trade, *Compendium of Living Wage Declarations and Reports*, 1922.

New South Wales, *Parliamentary Debates*, 1900, 1901, 1908, 1911, 1912, 1918, 1919, 1920, 1922.

New South Wales, *Parliamentary Papers*, vol. i, 1913.

New South Wales Royal Commission, *Report of Inquiry into the Working of Compulsory Conciliation and Arbitration Laws*, 1901.

New South Wales Statutes, 1901, No. 59; 1908, No. 3 and No. 24; 1912, No 17; 1916, No. 81; 1918, No. 16 and 39; 1919, No. 50; 1920, No. 19; 1922, No. 30.

Queensland, *Industrial Gazette*, 1917-1925.

Queensland *Statutes*, 1908, 1912, 1916, 1923, 1924.

South Australia, *Statutes*, 1890, 1894, 1912, 1915, 1916, 1920, No. 1453.

Victorian Employers' Federation, *Compulsory Arbitration, A Case against Them*, 1901.

Victoria, *Statutes*, 1896, no. 1445; 1898, no. 1598; 1900, no. 1645; 1905, no. 1975; 1910, no. 2305; 1914, no. 2558.

INDEX

Adamson Law, 45, 173-179, 201
Alabama, 14
Allen, Governor, 32, 40-42
Arbitration,
  Act of 1888, U. S., 55-56;
  defined, 11;
  principles of, 202-206, 209-215
Australia, Commonwealth of, 147, 189-199, 201
California, 14, 15-16
Canada, Compulsory Investigation Act of, 103-126, 201
Cohen, Judge, 177
Colorado, 14, 26-28, 200
Connecticut, 14
Coolidge, President, 98
Davis, John W., 99
Definitions, 10-13
Erdman Act, 57-69
Georgia, 14, 17
Gompers, Samuel, 39-40
Harding, President, 96-98
Heydon, Judge, 179
Higgins, H. B., 192
Huggins, William L., 32, 35-37
Howell-Barkley bill, 100-102
Idaho, 14
Illinois, 14, 15
Indiana, 14, 15
Investigation,
  defined, 12;
  principles, 206-209
Iowa, 14, 54
Kansas, 14, 30-53, 54, 200
Knights of Labor, 56
Louisiana, 14
Maine, 14
Marshall, Alfred, 146
Maryland, 14, 15
Mediation, definition of, 11
Minnesota, 14
Montana, 14
Nebraska, 14
Nevada, 14
New Hampshire, 14
New Jersey, 14, 54
Newlands Act, 69-72
New South Wales, compulsory arbitration system of, 157, 158, 159-181
New York, 14, 19-20, 54, 200
New Zealand, Alliance of Labor, 140;
  compulsory arbitration system of, 127-146, 147, 152, 201;
  Employers' Federation, 144
Ohio, 14, 20-23, 54, 200
Oregon, 14
Oklahoma, 14
Pennsylvania, 14, 18-19, 54, 200
Queensland, 157, 158, 174, 181-189
South Australia, 147-151, 157, 158
South Carolina, 14, 28-30
South Dakota, 14
Tasmania, 147, 151-2, 157, 158
Texas, 14
Transportation Act, 82-102
United States R. R. Labor Board, 84-102
Utah, 14
Vermont, 14
Victoria, wage board system of, 152-159, 174
Walsh, Frank P., 37-38
Washington, 14
Western Australia, 157-158
Wilson, President, 87-89
Wisconsin, 14

Bei Fragen zur Produktsicherheit wenden Sie sich bitte an:
If you have any questions regarding product safety,
please contact:

Walter de Gruyter GmbH
Genthiner Straße 13
10785 Berlin
productsafety@degruyterbrill.com